Latino
Visions

Latino Visions

Visions

Contemporary Chicano, Puerto Rican, and Cuban American Artists

By James D. Cockcroft assisted by Jane Canning

FRANKLIN WATTS

A Division of Grolier Publishing

New York London Hong Kong Sydney

Danbury, Connecticut

Photographs © ACA Galleries, New York: 36; Art Resource, NY: 37 (Gift of Frank K. Ribelin, National Museum of American Art, Smithsonian Institution, Washington DC), 81 (Teodoro Vidal Collection, National Museum of American Art, Smithsonian Institution, Washington DC); Carmen Lomas Garza: 32 (Nicolas and Cristina Hernandez Trust Collection, Pasadena, CA, photo by M. Lee Fatheree), 59 (Bob Hsiang); Christie's Images: 65 (ARS), cover top left, 70 (Private Collection, Miami, FL, Courtesy of George Adams Gallery, NY); Commonarts: 34 bottom (Ray Patlan, Anna DeLeon, Osha Neuman and Brian Thiele); Corbis-Bettmann: 98; Courtesy of Gloria Delson Contemporary Arts: 38; Courtesy of Jeff Adkisson and Luis Manuel Del Pilar: 67 (Bruce White/Miami Art Museum); Eva Cockcroft: 43; Fonda del Sol, Washington, DC: 71; Galería Botello, PR: 64, 85 (John Betancourt); George Adams Gallery, New York: 112 (eeva-inkeri), 97 (John Betancourt/Galería Botello, PR), 117, 120, 110 (Judy Cooper), 39 (Collection of the Hirshhorn Museum, Washington, D.C.), 69 top (Private Collection, Miami); James Cockcroft: 30; Juan Sanchez: 88 (David Dilley), cover top right, 66; Maria Brito: 69 bottom, 68; Museum of History, Anthropology and Art of the University of Puerto Rico: 82; Ramon Jose Lopez: 15; Rupert Garcia: 35 top; Social and Public Art Resource Center, Venice, CA: cover bottom, 34 top, 35 bottom, 49; Victor Ochoa: 33; William F. Herron III, 1972: 44.

Book design by Vicki Fischman

Visit Franklin Watts on the Internet at:
http://publishing.grolier.com

Library of Congress Cataloging-in-Publication Data

Cockcroft, James D.
Latino visions: contemporary Chicano, Puerto Rican, and Cuban American artists / by James D. Cockcroft ; assisted by Jane Canning.
    p. cm.
Includes bibliographical references and index.
    Summary: Describes the evolution of Latino art in America through discussion of variousartistic movements and important Latino artists.
    ISBN 0-531-11312-4 (lib. bdg.)   0-531-16523-X (pbk.)
    1. Hispanic American art—Juvenile literature. 2. Art, Modern—20th Century—United States—Juvenile literature. [1. Hispanic American art. 2. Art, Modern—20th Century. 3. Art appreciation. 4. Artists. 5. Hispanic Americans—Biography.] I. Cockcroft, James D. II. Title.

N6538.H58 C63 2000
704.03'68073—dc21
99-089464

Contents

Introduction

What is Latino art? Is it just a label for artworks made by Spanish-speaking people living in the United States? No, Latino art tells the exciting story of Latino, American Indian, and other peoples who, through historical accident, became part of the United States. It especially portrays people from today's American Southwest and Mexico, the Caribbean, and Central and South America. Latino art captivates us by its striking imagination, beauty, and universal range. It is truly an expression of different peoples and cultures.

Latinos are a growing part of the U.S. population today. We hear the Spanish language and Latino rhythms everywhere. Salsa has become more popular than ketchup on our kitchen tables. Just as Latinos have played a role in U.S. history and politics, sports, and music, they have also enriched our American heritage by bringing us a world of beauty and magic, of love of family and community, of humor and wit, and a deeper appreciation of nature and the spiritual side of life. Latino artists give us their visions of the past and the present in their paintings, murals, art installations, sculptures, posters, and performances.

These artists come from all walks of life. Some are carpenters, others are students, and a few are priests, but they all share a common language and values that unite them in the fertile ground of their heritage. They honor the rich traditions of their ancestors, the struggles of their people, and the power of the human spirit. Through their art, they express the beauty of legends and dreams in a celebration of their cultures, their people, and indeed, of all people.

Sometimes when we think of art, we think of quiet museums and imposing galleries, of famous artists who are long dead. Latino artists have a strong commitment to making art a part of public life, whether in the home, on the side of a building, or at a bus stop. It is art to be seen and enjoyed by everyone.

Today, there is more attention than ever before being paid to the work of Latino artists. Many museums are actively seeking out and presenting their work. Mexican artist Frida Kahlo has become a hugely popular figure, and Colombian Fernando Botero's work is increasingly well known.

Not too long ago, though, Latino art—whether created by artists in Latin America, the United States or, like Botero, in Europe—was thought to be too flashy, too political, or merely "folk art." To be sure, occasional controversial artists attracted attention and acclaim—such as *Los Tres Grandes* (The Three Greats): Mexico's muralists Diego Rivera, David Siqueiros, and

José Clemente Orozco. Others, including modern masters like Cuban artist Wifredo Lam and Chilean artist Roberto Matta, achieved recognition in the United States only after they had established reputations in Europe. Others seemed to be invisible, like Rafael Tufiño of Puerto Rico, who remained unrecognized by those "fine art" institutions that tell us what should and should not be called "art."

In fact, until the 1980s, exhibits by Latinos usually remained on the sidelines or in alternative gallery spaces. Racism, stereotyping of Latinos, and a refusal to recognize some of the art forms used by Latino artists as "art" contributed to this shocking state of affairs.

During the 1960s and 1970s, on the nation's streets and in its schools, Latino artists in the United States began to explore and discover and express the rich legacy of their cultures. They explored the legends, goddesses and gods of the ancient Pueblo, Aztec, and Mayan Indian civilizations; the rituals and myths of the Taino Indians; the African spirit rituals of the *Santería* religions; and the unwritten history of their own families in building the United States of America. They brought the magnificent and proud culture of Latino peoples to life through the arts.

At the same time, Latino artists mobilized to bring art to the people. They put up posters and painted graffiti and murals on the walls of buildings, houses, school cafeterias, and even on the pillars of highway overpasses. Much of their eye-catching work depicted the struggles of ordinary people, their suffering and courage in the face of discrimination and injustice. Stories of exile, immigration, and oppression continue to be told through these art forms.

Inevitably, this movement in art caught the attention of the museum world. In 1977, the alternative gallery Fondo Del Sol Arts Center in Washington, D.C., organized the first national touring exhibition of Latino artists in major museums. Several other major art institutions then began showcasing the work of Latino artists for mainstream audiences.

Today, major museums throughout the United States hold large Latino art collections. These include the National Museum of American Art in Washington, D.C., which has promoted important work by Latino artists and features many examples in its permanent collection. There are also museums devoted exclusively to Latino art, such as the Museum of Contemporary Hispanic Art and the Museo del Barrio in New York City, the Mexican Museum in San Francisco, La Plaza de la Raza in Los Angeles, and the Cuban Museum of Arts and Culture in Miami.

The attention and recognition that Latino artists have received still falls short of their contributions, and the snobbish attitude toward much of Latino art continues. Many books on American art highlight the works of a select few Latino artists, such as Kahlo or Rivera, but remain silent on other great works by more contemporary Latino artists.

Labeling works by Latino artists as "Latino art" is itself becoming a matter of debate among artists and the arts community in general. The politics of the art world and the use of ethnic or gender labels to define art make it hard for some artists to be successful and still be true to their vision. As Latino artists become more accepted by the mainstream culture, however, they may find themselves freer to express their ideas in ways that reflect their unique style without worrying about labels put on them by the art establishment.

This book celebrates the artworks of three large groups of Latinos living on the mainland of the United States: the Chicanos (or Mexican Americans), the Puerto Ricans, and the Cuban Americans. Naturally, not every artist or artwork can be mentioned in a short book intended to introduce readers to the world of Latino art. This book provides selected examples rather than an exhaustive compendium. The works presented or discussed here are aesthetically brilliant, often intricate, and always powerful. They weave a complex, moving, and human story.

To enter the world of Latino art, we must embark on a journey through the shrouded mists of time to a place where ancient gods, rain forests, and deserts alive with animal and nature spirits watch over our dreams and our nightmares. We must enter a space somewhere between heaven and earth, where ordinary people live, work, and laugh together.

The Art of the Southwest: Saints that Speak

Although it is scarcely mentioned in the history of American art, one of the oldest artistic traditions in the United States is that of the *santeros* (saint makers). It is alive and well in the Southwestern states, thanks in large part to the strength of Latino beliefs and the great respect given to spiritual traditions.

In 1492, when the Spanish explorers arrived in search of gold and glory, they brought their culture and religion with them. Their missionaries set about converting the Pueblo, Pima, Apache, and Chichimec peoples to the Roman Catholic faith. Churches sprang up to serve the growing communities of colonists and converts. The geographical remoteness of the region soon forced the Spaniards to make their own supplies—furniture, clothing, and religious objects to fill the newly constructed missions. Relying on their own creativity and inspiration, the self-taught Spanish painters and carvers used the available materials native to the landscape to produce the beautiful statues and painted images known as *santos* (saints).

They and their descendants are the proud product of a mixture of blood and heritage that shapes this *santero* artistic tradition. Carved statues of saints and holy personages, such as Christ on the cross, are known as *bultos*, while paintings on flat pieces of wood, metal, or animal skin are called *retablos*. The art of the *santero* is an original American art form that, despite almost dying out, has survived for over four hundred years as the love and knowledge of saint making has passed from generation to generation.

The oldest surviving examples of the work of the *santeros* are sacred images painted on animal hides. By 1999, only twenty-six such hides had been preserved. The early *santeros* used berries, herbs, bark, and minerals to make their paint. Their brushes were made from plant fibers, horsehair, and human hair. They carved the *santos* out of pine, cottonwood, aspen, and other local trees, and made their own hand tools. The finished figures were coated in a varnish made from piñon sap. The resulting objects were beautiful and powerful, and, unlike figures imported from Europe, they were made available to everyone for community or home worship. *Santeros* also carved altar screens that adorned churches with their intricate renderings of holy images.

Much of the work of the early *santeros* was lost in the Great Pueblo Revolt of 1680, when American Indians rebelled against the Spaniards and ordered the destruction of despised symbols of Spanish rule, including many sacred images. Some historians suggest the *santos* were targeted for destruction because many rebel leaders believed in the power of these objects. Scholars have pointed out that many ordinary American Indians saved the *santos* by pretending to damage and destroy them, and then hiding them.

The re-establishment of Spanish rule in 1692 meant the comeback of the *santeros.* Over the next 150 years, splendid painted carvings and screens adorned chapels throughout the Southwest. One of the most famous *santeros,* José Rafael Aragón, filled many churches with his work. The statues of saints became objects of great devotion and reflected the harsh life of the Spanish pioneer settlers.

One such statue of a saint, which continues to be a favorite today was that of San Ysidro, the patron of agriculture and farming. Another beloved figure was Our Lady of Guadalupe, an image of the Virgin Mary of Mexican origin, known as the protector of people of Indian ancestry. Traditionally, these images were carried in ceremonial processions through the fields at harvest time to bring good fortune to the community.

Ramón José López **San Ysidro** *1991*

The year 1821 marked a turning point in the history of the Southwest. Mexico declared its independence from Spain and at the same time, the Santa Fe Trail paved the way for waves of English-speaking settlers pushing westward. Thousands of the new arrivals, called "Anglos" by the locals, settled in what is now the southwestern United States. Like the Spaniards before them, they tried to impose their values, language, and culture on the local people. The Spanish-speaking population, which could claim American Indian as well as Spanish heritage, saw their land and their way of life threatened by this new European conquest, particularly after the U.S.–Mexico War (1846–1848). U.S. military forces and local judges enforced decisions that robbed them of their properties and ridiculed their customs, while tolerating or encouraging lynchings, rapes, and beatings of anyone who resisted.

The Anglo authorities of the Roman Catholic Church decided the *bultos, retablos,* and altar screens were "pagan" and ordered them to be destroyed. Most Mexicans, seeing their culture under siege, resisted the Anglo efforts at "cultural cleansing." Attempts to discourage the *santeros* and the use of *santos* sometimes met with violence, as people tried to protect the *santos* from those who regarded them as false idols. An additional threat to the *santeros* came from the introduction of cheap, mass-produced plaster religious statues and lithographs. Since the official Catholic priests took such a dim view of Mexican religious customs, some of the Mexicans turned to the Penitente Brotherhood, a grassroots movement of the Catholic people that attempted to keep their traditions and ceremonies alive. Brotherhood followers rescued many sacred objects by hiding them in people's homes.

Operating on their own, the Brotherhood practiced their faith in village communities. And, protected by the Brotherhood and the community, *santeros* continued to produce their art. Many of the finest pieces were produced during the second half of the nineteenth century and the early twentieth century. José Benito Ortega, one of the great *santeros* of the time, created more than two hundred pieces.

Today's *santeros*, like their predecessors, are enjoying recognition and respect. These artists all work in the traditional manner, some using methods and materials handed down through the generations. Just as important to their art are the spiritual values that saint making involves. As one noted *santero* simply affirms, "To create images of saints you must have a deep sense of family and faith. Otherwise they will not be able to achieve the sense of spirituality that the work must possess."[1]

A younger *santero* explains this in a different way: "In Latin American culture, there's a belief that *santos* [saints] can help you in your life. By respecting those traditions, creating a *santo* is actually like saying a prayer to that specific saint. The faith is what inspires us to create."[2]

Artist Cruz López explains one of his works, *Our Lady of Sorrows* (a favorite image among the Penitente Brotherhood), in terms of his own life. "It really means a lot to me because I identify very much with the sorrow that she felt. I can somehow understand it and put myself in her place. It's a way to think about things because you spend so much time perfecting the artwork. In this way, I feel like I become closer to God."[3] Like so many others, Cruz López comes from a long line of *santeros*. However, many other *santeros* do not. They rely on the models of works by earlier *santeros* and on their own mastery of traditional techniques.

Ramón José López
Born 1951, Santa Fe, New Mexico

For López, art is a family affair. He is the grandson of Lorenzo López, a *santero* who died two years before Ramón José was born. While the two never met, Ramón José has explored his grandfather's legacy, making *santos* following the New Mexican folk tradition. López also uses many of his grandfather's tools in Spanish colonial metalworking, making traditional silver objects, such as candelabras and chalices. López creates many types of traditional religious objects, such as reliquaries, which are decorated containers made for holding religious relics. In recent years, López has also explored the art of painting on buffalo hide. A traveling exhibit, "Cuando Hablan Los Santos" (When the Saints Speak), includes the work of López and his four children, who continue the family artistic traditions.

Another contemporary artist who carries on his *santero* heritage is Ramón José López. In 1997, he was awarded a National Heritage Fellowship by the National Endowment for the Arts. He uses methods handed down from his grandfather and, in turn, has passed this knowledge on to his own children. He believes that the making of *santos* is an expression of his faith and his heritage.

> *My traditional work let me see how influenced I really was by my heritage, my history. It showed me my roots in this area—it opened my eyes. It's all inspired by my upbringing here, my Catholic religion, and my interest in the churches of New Mexico with their beautiful altar screens. I want to achieve the quality of these old masters . . . what they captured on wood, emotions so powerful, so moving.*[4]

Chicanos: Aztlán and Larger Visions

By laying claim to the past, many artists—and not just the *santeros*—hope to better understand the present and learn where their own roots lie. During the 1960s, the awakening of the Chicano movement involved issues of self-identity, religion, art, music, theater, education, and dress, as well as a political struggle for civil rights. The search of young Chicanos for images and symbols that expressed the ideas of self-identity, resistance, and survival led them to explore ancient mythology and religion to discover the spiritual side unique to the Chicano people—the descendants of Mexicans. At the same time, Chicano families in the United States struggled for survival, facing harsh working conditions endured by migrant agricultural workers in the rural areas and the dangers of everyday *barrio* life—drugs, gangs, police brutality—in the inner cities.

One of these struggles centered on the Chicano and Filipino farmworkers, who cultivated and harvested California's huge crops of wine and table grapes. Their efforts to form a labor union and negotiate for better working conditions became a national cause backed by a consumer boycott of California grapes. The workers' symbol, the thunderbird with the union logo of *Huelga!* (Strike!)—was often incorporated into the artwork of that period. The success of the farmworkers' strike finally brought better job and educational opportunities, access to schools and health care, and an end to the heavy use of poisonous pesticides in the crop fields.

An important part of this struggle went beyond obtaining basic human rights. As Chicano poet Rudolfo Anaya observed, "Our existence as a group was threatened by Anglicization [cultural cleansing] which was real in the 1960s. But it was also a time of heightened spiritual awareness, of our relationship to the gods—giving us a sense of purpose and destiny. . . . These times are marked by a renaissance in the arts."[1]

Chicano artists became a forceful presence. Painters, sculptors, muralists, and performance artists, Chicanos and Chicanas (male and female Mexican Americans), raised their voices in a celebration of their culture and traditions, often portraying everyday life in extraordinary ways.

Figures in their artwork—whether grandmothers, fruit vendors, or grape pickers—are portrayed in proud and powerful images. Many Chicano artists draw inspiration from a rich and ancient past: the pre-Colombian civilizations of the Aztec, Toltec, and Maya Indians. As a group, Chicanos can claim direct descent from the American Indian peoples of Mexico and the United States and the Spanish settlers. Some of their ancestors actually lived in the United States long before the arrival of the "Anglos" at Plymouth Rock.

Despite this proud heritage, the Chicano people have often been persecuted and excluded from the "American Dream," struggling to make a living in a hostile environment. For this reason, many Chicano artists choose themes of resistance and struggle for their works. A mixture of blood and history is an integral part of the Chicano experience, and Chicano artists draw on these roots to bring art to the Chicano community.

An important part of the Chicano artistic renaissance is the mural movement, along with a rediscovery of traditional art such as the *santos*. As artists stepped up to meet the challenges of the 1960s and early 1970s, they saw their works as a way to express what it means to be Chicano. The quest for an authentic identity and the reclaiming of ancient traditions were not merely nostalgia trips. Through their art and murals, Chicano artists could bring to life ancient gods and goddesses, forgotten heroes and heroines, and remind people of their proud heritage, a heritage that had been erased by centuries of European occupation. Using these older symbols, the artists told the story of their ancestors and their accomplishments, giving Chicanos an opportunity to take pride in their common roots. As the poet Alurista explains: "There was a need for all of us to find a way . . . that would serve as a unifying tool to look at each other as brothers and sisters."[2]

The idea of Chicano unity that inspired many artists of the time was symbolized by the mythical land of origin for Chicanos— *Aztlán*. The land was said to be located in the southwestern United States and considered to be the true Chicano homeland. Aztlán became an inspirational symbol for Chicano art, writing, poetry, and politics. Whether real or imaginary, Aztlán was said to exist in the hearts and minds of all who claim to be its descendants. So, under the banner of Aztlán, all Chicanos could share a common heritage, in spite of their obviously different experiences as immigrants and eighth-generation U.S. citizens, rural laborers and city dwellers, West-coasters and East-coasters.

Under the Treaty of Guadalupe Hidalgo in 1848, which ended the U.S.–Mexico War, and the 1854 Gadsden Purchase, Mexico ceded to the United States the land that is now the states of Texas, Arizona, California, Utah, and parts of Colorado, Nevada, and Wyoming. Although the treaty stated clearly that all Mexican residents of the newly acquired U.S. territories were guaranteed full rights as U.S. citizens, the reality was that Mexicans and their children were treated like exiles in their own land, becoming "foreigners," or "aliens," without ever leaving the land of their birth.

From 1848 to World War I (1914–1918) and after, Mexican Americans and hundreds of thousands of Mexicans imported to work in the mines, farms, and factories of the United States, were harshly treated. Many Mexican American families in the Southwest were forced off their farms and ranches, denied schooling, and subjected to racist attacks. It is estimated that from 1850 to 1930, the number of Mexican Americans and Mexicans killed in racist attacks in the Southwest exceeded the number of African-Americans lynched in the South.

Only through art, music, and tradition could Chicanos keep their self-respect and preserve their true history. *Corridos,* ballads passed down from generation to generation, tell stories of confrontations with the Anglo world. Many of the events recorded in these songs were violent. For example, the "Ballad of Gregorio Cortez" recounts a true story from 1900 of a man who, because of a linguistic misunderstanding, is wrongfully accused of stealing a horse. After shooting an Anglo sheriff in self-defense, the man flees for his life, chased by a huge force of Texas Rangers, a special police force created to protect settlers from bandits, but which also harassed Mexicans and Chicanos. Cortez becomes a social hero for all underdogs. In 1982, actor James Edward Olmos starred in a Chicano film production of the story, *The Ballad of Gregorio Cortez.*

The expansion of modern industry that brought job opportunities in U.S. cities led to the Mexican immigration that started in the 1890s and continued into the mid-1950s. These developments, combined with the forces of racism, caused Chicanos to settle in segregated urban communities called barrios. Increasingly, Chicanos found themselves in direct contact with Anglo society—in workplaces, on city streets, and in some of the schools. The resultant clash of cultures brought forth the need to define what it means to be Chicano and the need to preserve traditionally held values as well as to fight for equal rights in housing, education, and the workplace. In California's public schools, Mexican Americans won court cases against racial segregation in

1931 (Lemon Grove) and 1946–1947 (Westminster), helping to pave the way for the law against school segregation in 1954 (a Supreme Court decision that ironically did not apply to Mexican Americans and other Latinos until 1973).[3]

Eventually, Chicano artists united to respond to these challenges, rallying entire communities to join in collective expressions of Chicano pride through what became known as the mural movement. The arts became a peaceful weapon in the larger struggle for social justice.

Into the Streets: Up Against the Wall

The Chicano mural movement sprang from the heart of the Chicano community, unleashing creative energy that, until the late 1960s, had not found a satisfactory outlet to express the Chicano experience. The walls and alleyways of Chicano barrios became a superhighway for artistic expression.

Looking for a way to create art of the people and for the people, Chicano artists found a natural solution in murals. After all, mural art was already part of an established Mexican tradition, harking back to *Los Tres Grandes* (The Three Greats)—Diego Rivera, David Siqueiros, and José Clemente Orozco. In the 1920s and 1930s, these great artists had gained international fame for their powerful painted murals of historic events. Many fine examples of their work were created in the United States, including those of Rivera in San Francisco, Siqueiros in Los Angeles, and Orozco in Claremont, California. Wealthy U.S. patrons of the arts hired them to paint huge public murals. Some of these murals created a lot of controversy because of their strong portrayal of

Diego Rivera

Born 1886, Guanajuato, Mexico • Died 1957, Mexico City

Rivera, who began to draw at the age of three, became the most well-known modern Mexican mural painter. Rivera used his murals to express revolutionary themes, and his work in the United States influenced socially conscious American artists of the Depression era who created hundreds of murals for public buildings under federally funded art programs.

Rivera studied at the Academia de San Carlos in Mexico City from 1898 to 1905, and in 1906 received a scholarship to study in Europe. He traveled to Spain, France, Belgium, England, and Italy. When he returned to Mexico in 1921, his large mural works reflected his view of the struggles between the social classes. In his early mural projects, Rivera concentrated on social and political themes, such as the murals at the National Preparatory School in 1922 and the Ministry of Education Building in 1923 through 1928, both in Mexico City. As his popularity grew, he received invitations to paint murals at the San Francisco Stock Exchange in 1931, the Detroit Institute of Art in 1932, and Rockefeller Center in New York City in 1933. His art has been exhibited in many museums throughout the United States, Mexico, and England.

political themes of social justice. Rivera's mural at the Detroit Institute for the Arts was labeled "un-American" and triggered a public outcry to have it destroyed, while his next mural at New York City's Rockefeller Center was in fact destroyed on orders from its sponsor, billionaire John D. Rockefeller.

The vicious racial slurs directed at Orozco's *Epic of American Civilization* at Dartmouth College typified the attitude of some critics of the time. They mocked his depiction of ancient Aztec gods as "hideous divinities of Mexico . . . and the extremely tiresome tradition of an absent and somewhat abhorred civilization of the Toltec-Aztec cults." The controversies stirred up by Mexi-

José Clemente Orozco

Born 1883, Zapotlan, Mexico • Died 1949, Mexico City

Orozco, one of Mexico's most important mural painters, moved with his family from Zapotlan, Mexico, to Mexico City, in 1890. He studied agriculture before turning to painting in 1909. During the early years of the Mexican Revolution, Orozco worked as a cartoonist and illustrator for several politically radical newspapers. He painted his first mural in 1922 and, over the next five years, decorated the walls of several public buildings, including the National Preparatory School and the House of Tiles in Mexico City. From 1927 through 1934, Orozco traveled in the United States where he painted several frescoes, including a fresco at the New School for Social Research in New York City. Upon his return to Mexico, he created several major works, such as his *Man in His Four Aspects: the Worker, the Educator, the Creative Thinker, the Rebel*, and his famous *The Man of Fire* mural, completed in 1939. Orozco's style reflected his deep feelings for the poor and oppressed. His work has been exhibited in many museums throughout the world, including the United States, England, and Germany.

David Alfaro Siqueiros

Born 1896, Chihuahua, Mexico • Died 1974, Cuernavaca, Mexico

Siqueiros was one of Mexico's leading twentieth-century painters. His art reflected his commitment to socialism and revolution. During the Mexican Revolution of 1910, he contributed to the revolutionary newspaper *La Vanguardia.* He joined the revolutionary forces, and later traveled to Europe as a military attaché where he met Diego Rivera in Paris. In 1921, he edited the Barcelona review *Vida Americana*, which advocated monumental public art, indigenous culture, and the need to blend universal themes with new forms and modern materials. After returning to Mexico City in 1922, Siqueiros painted murals at the National Preparatory School and began fresco commissions in Los Angeles at the Chouinard School of Art and the Plaza Art Center in 1932. In 1936, Siqueiros went to New York City where he established an experimental workshop that explored the use of modern industrial tools and paints, photography, and "accidental methods" in the fine arts. He completed murals in Chillán, Chile, in 1942, and Havana, Cuba, in 1943, and from 1952 to 1958 painted murals in Mexico City, including those at the Ciudad Universitaria and at the Museo Nacional de Historia. His more important works include those in the Palace of Fine Arts and the National University of Mexico in Mexico City, and his masterpiece, finished in 1968, *The March of Humanity in Latin America,* also in Mexico City. Siqueiros received the National Prize from the Mexican government in 1966 and the Lenin Peace Prize from the Soviet Union in 1967.

can mural art brought some people's racist attitudes into the headlines. They viewed Mexican artists as "Indians" who could not possibly meet the standards of "European-American civilization." Even Orozco, born in Mexico after his parents had emigrated from Spain, a European country, was still labeled "dull" and working class.

Siqueiros's 1932 *America Tropical* mural in the Mexican barrio of East Los Angeles provoked an outcry because of its portrayal of a crucified Mexican immigrant. A third of its surface was painted over in 1934 and the rest of it was painted over in 1938. It would have been lost to history if the Chicano mural movement had not come along so many decades later, reawakening interest in the works of earlier great muralists. In late 1998, Jewish-American muralist Eva Cockcroft and Mexico-born Latina muralist Alessandra Moctezuma and their assistants re-painted the mural on another wall in East Los Angeles with additional panels of their own as a *Homage to Siqueiros*. Their work won the Mural of the Month Award. Artist Cockcroft died of breast cancer a few months later, and was widely honored for her contributions to Latino art and the worldwide mural movement. At the mural's dedication fiesta, mariachi musicians played, people danced, and television cameras whirred, but the mass media saw fit not to report the story or even show a single shot of the *Homage to Siqueiros* mural on television. The image of the crucified immigrant was still considered too controversial.

Yet for the previous thirty years, hundreds upon hundreds of murals had been popping up on walls and buildings throughout the Southwest, the Midwest, and indeed the entire United

Artists Eva Cockcroft and Alessandra Moctezuma stand near their mural **Homage to Siqueiros** *1998.*

States. They decorated barrio landscapes with dramatic images of heroes and saints, Aztec and Mayan gods, and political protesters, as well as ordinary people and scenes of barrio life. The Chicano artists were battling negative images and stereotypes of Chicanos and Mexicans as lazy, dirty, and ignorant. Turning inward to their own communities, these artists found a way to celebrate Chicano culture in scenes of daily life. Their art presented the history and experiences of the Chicano people as a proud and strong example.

Teams of Chicano muralists and young people, working mainly in the cities of the Southwest and Midwest, turned walls, buildings, highway ramps, parks, and other public spaces into a huge canvas of images celebrating *La Raza*—all things Chicano and, by extension, all of the human race. In San Diego, for instance, the Centro Cultural de la Raza had impressive murals at its headquarters and on a large water tank in Balboa Park. Víctor Ochoa's mural *Geronimo* covers part of the Centro's wall with a powerful image of the Apache warrior painted as a proud freedom fighter, with whom Ochoa identifies as a comrade in the struggle for Chicano community rights. And down by the bay, nearly a hundred murals were painted on bridge support pillars in San Diego's Logan barrio, rebaptized *Chicano Park*.

Some of the mural painters were professionally trained, others were high school dropouts, or "pushouts" as they called themselves, because schools discriminated against them. They had been placed in the least desirable courses where little could be learned and career opportunities were limited. Chicano mural art juxtaposes images of low-rider cars, graffiti, tattoos, and *pachuco* (zoot suit) styles with family portraits and kids in sneakers playing soccer. The murals often lash out with an in-your-face *rasquache* feeling—a brazen, garish, outrageous quality, a kind of "good taste–poor taste" statement easily identified by its style, whether done with spray paint cans or with a brush.

At the same time, the search for roots and identity led many artists to include images from Mexican history. Some works showed revolutionary heroes, such as Emiliano Zapata and Pancho Villa, and gods, goddesses, and heroes from the Maya, Aztec, Toltec, and Apache civilizations. A good example of these themes can be found in Estrada Courts—a public-housing project in East Los Angeles—where a huge likeness of the Aztec rain god Tlaloc shares space with Mayan stone carvings.

Sometimes ancient symbols are combined with Catholic figures such as Mexico's patroness saint, the Virgin of Guadalupe. Often this figure is shown in updated modern versions. One example is the triptych of the *Virgin of Guadalupe* by Yolanda López, who takes the traditional cloak of stars and body halo for herself and her mother and grandmother. Her mother, an ancient Indian woman, is seated at a sewing machine, and the artist herself is the Virgin of Guadalupe decked out in running shoes as she bursts through the frame cloaked like a superwoman. In another depiction, Ester Hernández's etching shows the Virgin in karate attire *Defending the rights of Chicanos.* The ever present *rasquache* attitude, caused this work to be criticized for using a sacred image in such a way.

The dilemmas of immigration, deportation, and achieving the "American Dream" are the subject matter of the poster art of many Chicano artists, including Malaquías Montoya and Rupert García. Montoya's black-and-white silk-screen poster *Abajo con la migra* (Down with the Migra . . . Stop Deportation) shows the statue of liberty with the body of a Latina immigrant impaled on the points of its crown and surrounded by strands of barbed wire.

Carmen Lomas Garza
El Milagro
1987

Oil on canvas
36 × 48 in.
(91 × 122 cm)

Víctor Ochoa

Geronimo

Acrylic on concrete

1981

70 ✕ 22 ft.

(178 ✕ 56 cm)

Mario Torero

Virgen de Guadalupe

1978

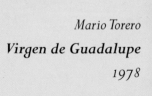

DIVISION OF THE BARRIOS & CHAVEZ RAVINE

Judith F. Baca

Division of the Barrios & Chavez Ravine, *1983*

13 1/2 ✕ 20 foot section from The Great Wall of Los Angeles 1978–83 (4 x 6 m)

Commonarts

Song of Unity, *1978*

30 ✕ 20 ft. (9 ✕ 6 m)

Rupert García
Cry of the Rebel
1975
Silk-screen print
26 × 20 in.
(66 × 51 cm)

Alma Lopez
Las Four
1997
Digital mural
8 × 9 ft.
(2 x 3 m)

Luis Jiménez
Vaquero
1987–88
Fiberglass
198 × 144 × 120 in.
(503 × 366 × 305 cm)

(above) *Carlos Almaraz*

Mystery in the Park
1989
Serigraph
34 1/2 ✕ 53 in. (88 ✕ 135 cm)

(left) Jesús Bautista Moroles
Granite Weaving
1988
Georgia gray granite
98 ✕ 74 1/2 ✕ 11 in. (249 ✕ 189 ✕ 28 cm)

Arnaldo Roche Rabell

Like a Thief in the Night, 1990

Oil on canvas

96 ✕ 96 in. (244 ✕ 244 cm)

The poster denounces the often ruthless tactics of the U.S. Immigration and Naturalization Service (*la migra*) in hunting down immigrants. García is a prolific artist who achieved mainstream status with a one-person show in the San Francisco Museum of Modern Art in 1978.

The 1970s–Gaining Recognition at Last

As the mural movement erupted, the traditional art establishment at first ignored it or ridiculed it. The movement's explosion of creativity found alternative, out-of-the-mainstream spaces for Chicano art. Community art galleries were formed, and artwork was also displayed in cultural centers, health clinics, and schools. Countless local organizations were formed to support the efforts of young artists. One of them, the Mechicano Art Center in Los Angeles, obtained money to transform the city's public bus stop benches into artistic sculpture. The Los Angeles Social and Public Art Resource Center (SPARC) was responsible for many of the murals that blanketed East Los Angeles in a river of images and colors.

San Francisco's Galería de la Raza, directed by artist René Yánez, showcased young talent and sparked several major murals in the city's Mission district during the early 1970s. Its confrontational tactics helped create an alternative for Latino artists who felt "shut out" by mainstream galleries and art critics. Emphasizing high professional standards, the gallery exhibited many artists who later became prominent, including Rupert García and Carmen Lomas Garza. It also generated countless high-quality silk-screen prints that, like the murals, were a form of public art with strong political messages. Emerging from the social and political turbulence of the 1960s, Chicano and other Latino printmakers and painters developed a powerful type of poster art that rooted itself in local communities and evoked the universal values of social justice and human solidarity.

Street art itself reached new heights under the influence of the Chicano and related Latino empowerment movements. In San Francisco's streets, groups such as the *Mujeres Muralistas* (Women Muralists) painted scenes depicting children, family values, the role of women in Chicano culture, and political struggle. In the barrios of Chicago, the Movimiento Artístico Chicano (MARCH) and Casa de Aztlán created murals, often with the assistance of local residents, especially teens. The Santa Fe-based Artes Guadalupanos de Aztlán combined the painting of huge striking images of Mexican gods and goddesses with political consciousness-raising in works like *Lady of Justice* and *Huitzitlopochtli*. These groups are just a few of the groups that formed the core of the Chicano mural movement and brought their art to neighborhoods across the United States.

Gradually, through the artworks themselves and books like *Toward a People's Art: The Contemporary Mural Movement* (1977, reissued 1998), this rich and powerful art commanded a national and international audience. As early as 1974, the Los Angeles County Museum of Art mounted a show by four professional Chicano artists known as *Los Four*—Carlos Almaraz, Robert de la Rocha, Gilbert Sánchez Luján, and Frank Romero. Los Four brought the barrio into the museum, collectively creating a special spray-paint mural. Their show, filled with graffiti and

Artes Guadalupanos de Aztlán **Huitzitlopochtli**

spray-paint techniques, introduced many museum visitors to powerful images of Chicano and Mexican immigrant culture, including low-riders and the struggles of farmworkers.

Almaraz entered the museum world fresh from two years of volunteer work for the United Farmworkers Union. With other emergent artists, he had painted graphic designs for El Teatro Campesino, a popular theater group of workers and professionals who performed plays across the United States to raise money for striking workers. El Teatro Campesino, founded in 1965, was led by Luis Valdez, a future Broadway playwright (*Zoot Suit*) and filmmaker (*La Bamba* and *Zoot Suit*), and a former member of the well-known San Francisco Mime Troupe.

Almaraz, like Frank Romero, went on to exhibit in major museums and galleries, as did many other talented artists who emerged from the mural and Chicano empowerment movements. By the late 1970s, the U.S. mural movement, which included several prominent African-American, Asian, and white artists, had become the driving force of mural art around the world. Its most original contribution was in linking art directly to struggles of the people—creating a vibrant and monumental public art known as "people's art."

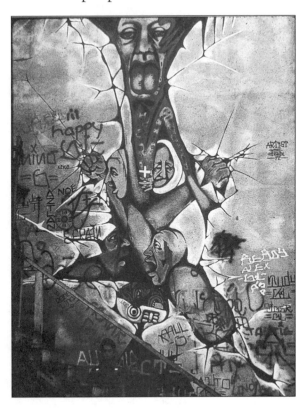

Willie F. Herrón Jr. **The Wall that Cracked Open** *1972   15 × 24 ft. (5 × 7 m)*

Some of the mural themes of the 1970s focused on the dangers of barrio life and the problems of drugs and gang violence. Artists wished to confront such threats to Chicano people. Willie F. Herrón Jr.'s mural *The Wall that Cracked Open* was painted in part to protest the attack on his brother by a rival gang. Among other images, it shows a beaten and bleeding youth with a weeping grandmother. It brilliantly incorporates actual cracks in the wall as well as the graffiti already on the wall along with the names inscribed there, treating them with respect. After painting the mural, the artist periodically returned to paint a small cross over the names of people on the wall when they died.

Santa Fe's Artes Guadalupanos de Aztlán painted their first mural in response to the death of a family member by drug overdose and the problem of heroin addiction in the barrio. They went on to create a series of murals with the help of recovering addicts. Many mural groups of the 1970s worked together with gang members and street people, especially in the cities of California and in Chicago.

Other groups, such as the Mujeres Muralistas of San Francisco, took a different approach, focusing on family life, children, love, and pride. "Our interest as artists is to put art close to where it needs to be; close to the children, close to the old people, close to everyone who has to walk or ride the buses to get places. We want our art either out on the streets or in places where a lot of people go each day, hospitals, health centers, clinics, restaurants, and other public places."[4] Juana Alicia, another Bay Area muralist and painter, took up the dangers of pesticides to women farmworkers in her 1983 *Las Lechugeras (The Lettuce Pickers)*, which shows pregnant workers exposed to pesticides. She explains that her concern is really about the need to protect the environment and the foods we eat. "I am committed to work towards peace and preserve the environment. I want my work to contribute to the transformation of a violent world into a humane one, reflecting the values of love."[5]

Perhaps the best-known organization involved in creating and documenting murals is the Social and Public Art Resource

Center of Los Angeles (SPARC) founded in 1976. SPARC murals have an estimated viewing audience of 1.2 million people every day and a long list of communities wait to participate. The president of SPARC affirms that "It is in the process of community collaboration that SPARC's greatest contribution is made. The finished work is secondary to the coming together of peoples who, until now have had no voice, no images, no monuments. Through this process they express their history, their frustrations, and their dreams."[6]

One of SPARC's most famous projects is *The Great Wall of Los Angeles*. More than 1/2 mile (0.8 kilometers) in length, it is the longest mural in the world. It tells the story of different minority groups and their important roles in California history. It was completed with the help of more than four hundred neighborhood youths and fifty artists who worked over five summers (1978–1983) to bring alive the untold history of Chinese, Japanese, Mexicans, African-Americans, women, immigrant workers, and other groups.

Different sections of *The Great Wall* mural show the women's suffrage movement, the Great Depression of the 1930s, the Japanese internment camps of World War II, the anti-Mexican "zoot suit riots," the birth of rock and roll featuring African-Americans like Chuck Berry, Olympic champions, and leaders of the civil rights movement. The "Division of the Barrios & Chavez Ravine" section of *The Great Wall* illustrate the struggles over building projects in poor parts of Los Angeles that forced people out of their homes and bulldozed entire neighborhoods. Many neighborhoods were cut up by highways. When

Dodger Stadium was built, residents were falsely promised new homes if they would leave. Others, like the woman shown in this part of the mural, fought to keep their homes, but were evicted by force. Judith Baca, SPARC's founder, said that the mural is really about developing harmony among ethnic groups and the cross-cultural understanding that can be achieved when people work together.

Beyond the Barrio

Chicano artists of the 1970s called for Chicano culture to be recognized as part of the history of the United States, as a culture that developed within its borders and on its borders. They created their images locally, but they soon found their work gaining national and international recognition. They themselves began thinking more globally and multiculturally.

An early sign of this more international and multiracial outlook appears in the Commonarts mural team's creation of the *Song of Unity* painted on the front of Berkeley's La Peña Cultural Center in 1978. The artists who painted the mural came from various racial and national backgrounds. One of them, Ray Patlán—like Baca, Herrón Jr., and so many others—is a widely recognized and prolific master muralist who is committed to community art. His murals can be seen around the San Francisco area, on the exterior of buildings, such as the deYoung Museum in Golden Gate Park and the Center for the Arts Complex at Yerba Buena Gardens. In 1994, Patlán designed murals for the World Cup Soccer competitions held in San Francisco. Chilean artists like Francisco Letelier and others have added their works to the proliferation of internationally minded murals in the United States. A later multicultural mural exemplifying the international trend is *Maestraspace*, a 1995 multiracial team mural involving Juana Alicia and impressively draping San Francisco's Women's Building. A group of seven women and their women supporters completed this incredible work.

Throughout the 1980s and 1990s, racial-harmony themes and global concerns emerged in Chicano artworks, while the muralists' links to local community bases continued. The mural *Doliente de Hidalgo* by Willie F. Herrón Jr., 1989–1990, tells the story of the Mexican struggle for freedom and independence from Spain. Father Miguel Hidalgo, the revolutionary priest who led the war of independence, is shown leading his followers. At the same time, the painting addresses the increase in Latin American contributions to the Los Angeles area.

SPARC's Neighborhood Pride program brought art into the poor neighborhoods of Los Angeles. It sponsored more than one hundred murals, always involving the community in the process while developing larger themes and visions. Some projects continue to celebrate Chicano themes along with international ones, such as Neighborhood Pride's *La Ofrenda* (The Offering), created by Yreina Cervántez in 1989 under Los Angeles' First Street Bridge. It is a tribute to farmworkers union organizer Dolores Huerta and honors the strength of Chicana and Central American women in the face of the hardships of immigration and war. The lower part of the mural was painted with spray cans by young artists from the neighboring Belmont Tunnel graffiti yard across the street.

Yreina Cervántez **La Ofrenda** *1989   16 × 52 ft. (5 × 16 m)*

SPARC's Neighborhood Pride also sponsored the 1990–1991 mural *Resurrection of the Green Planet* by Ernesto de la Loza. The mural speaks to our need to protect and preserve the environment. It calls for a true world community, respect for human rights, and appreciation for the cultures and contributions of all people and living things. The central image is a *curandera* (female healer or doctor), seen blessing a young person who is emerging from the earth. Symbols of fertility, harvest, growth, life, and rebirth appear throughout the mural. Above, angels represent earth, wind, and fire. The homeless and neglected are huddled in a corner. The artist explains: "At the foot of creativity there's destruction. If there's a central theme to this mural, it's how small the world is, how everything on this planet involves everybody."

In the mid-1990s, projects often used the latest in technology to create digital murals in urban neighborhoods. In 1997, Estrada Courts in East Los Angeles, a community known internationally for its colorful collection of Chicano murals, became the site for the latest technology in mural making: digitized photographs scanned onto murals that recount the history of the neighborhood. Known as "The Digital Murals," the SPARC-sponsored project was created by UCLA students who interviewed twenty-five local families and captured the emotions and social issues affecting their lives. "We wanted students to have the opportunity to do service-based learning," observed SPARC's Judith Baca. "It's important for them to not only learn about the arts in a theoretical way but to actually be involved in the real production of an artwork. It empowers students to understand how they create change in a community and improve the lives of the people they are in contact with."

The artists and students used computers to create collages out of pictures from family albums and other photographs. "The Digital Murals" illustrate the connections between individual lives, families, and the community. The "Las Four" section includes an image of a young woman and two elderly women surrounded by flowers. Behind them stands the image of a female saint. Other sections of the murals contain messages about taking pride in family and heritage. "These aren't images imposed from outside the community but are derived from interactive processes between the artists and the community," Baca said. "These murals symbolize the people's aspirations, their hopes and their worries."

The "World Wall" is a traveling mural exhibit based upon the theme of "A Vision of the Future Without Fear." Created by Baca, it was inspired by her conversations with Hopi elders. Monumental in scope, the mural is a series of painting on portable 30-foot (9.1-meter) high mural panels. It addresses the hopes and dreams of all people for world peace and harmony. The always evolving project has toured the United States and seven other countries, where new international panels have been added. They focus on issues of global concern: war, peace, interdependence, cooperation, and spiritual growth. In the great tradition of the Mexican muralists, this multi-paneled project seeks to connect the communities that make up what some have called the "global village."

Finding Success in the Mainstream

Like the Chicano muralists, artists working in other media have produced artworks that reflect the concerns of family values and traditions, portray barrio life, and present positive images of Mexican Americans and ordinary people as heroes. Some of these artists have become quite famous.

Luis Jiménez has received widespread acclaim during his thirty-year career as an artist. He is known primarily for his gigantic sculptures, which use pop culture to show the myths and media stereotypes of the Southwest. At the same time he draws on serious subjects such as war, immigration, and working people in the tradition of the mural movement. In fact, it has been said that Jiménez's art can be compared to the socially conscious works created for the federally sponsored Work Projects Administration (WPA) of the 1930s and the paintings by the great Mexican muralists of those years. "Jiménez shares a genuine concern for working people and those members of society who have suffered discrimination," observed Jay Gates, director of the Dallas Museum of Art, which has featured many of Jiménez's works over the years.[7]

Jiménez's background and experience served to shape his artistic outlook. Growing up in El Paso, Texas, during the 1950s, Jiménez came of age during the Vietnam War and the Chicano movement. He comes from a working-class family with a tradition of creativity. One of his grandfathers was a carpenter, the other a glassblower, and his father was a maker of neon signs. During his childhood, young Luis helped out in his father's shop, learning the skills he would use later by working with epoxy, fiberglass, and other materials that are now part of his trademark. These materials, more often connected with boat and car repairs, are molded and cast by Jiménez into huge shiny sculptures.

In his early work, Jiménez's fascination with cars and love of low-rider culture took aim at the myth of the "American Dream" and other American fantasies. *The American Dream* shows a nude, blonde, blue-eyed woman embracing a car. This standard of beauty bothered Jiménez. "Mexican Americans or anyone else who is not blonde or blue eyed is super aware of it because [you] don't fit this image."[8] In *The Barfly—Statue of Liberty* from 1969, at the height of the Vietnam War, the artist recalls, "I was making a very conscious attempt to make a social commentary about what I thought was going on in the country." The sculpture depicts a foxy blonde in a clingy tank top and miniskirt. She is perched on a bar stool, her arm stretched above her. In her left hand she holds a foamy beer mug. An American flag, with skulls instead of stars, flows from her bare thighs.

The 8-foot (2.4-m)-high *Man on Fire*, also dating from this period, is a majestic male figure, engulfed in bright red flames. In part it recalls the torture by fire of Cuauhtémoc, the last Aztec emperor to succumb in the Spanish invasion of Mexico. It also pays respect to the Buddhist monks who set themselves aflame to protest the invasion of Vietnam by the United States.

Later, Jiménez turned to the myths of the American West for his subject matter. His work encompassed giant wild horses and other figures of American folklore. *Vaquero* (Cowboy) is a larger-than-life gun-toting Mexican astride a bucking bronco. The artist gives us his take on the cowboy myth, explaining, "I was struck by the irony that our concept of the American cowboy was this John Wayne type image, this blond cowboy out of Hollywood, where in fact, the original cowboys were all Mexican. Somehow we'd lost sight of that." In *Southwest Pieta*, the European version of the Virgin Mary mourning the dead body of Christ is turned into a scene from Mexican mythology. It is a tale of forbidden love, with the two figures seated on a rock that is shared with a menacing bald eagle and a serpent.

In 1989, Jiménez completed a 10-foot (3-m)-high, totem-like sculpture to commemorate the experience of so-called "illegal aliens" and the anguish of the immigrant. Of this *Border Crossing (Cruzando El Río Bravo)*, Jiménez said: "People talked about the aliens as if they landed from outer space, as if they weren't really people. I wanted to put a face on them; I wanted to humanize them." In addition, he points out, he "wanted to deal with the whole idea of family. You see. . . . I had just started a new family. We had just had Adan. I went back to my experiences in El Paso where this figure is a common sight. The men carry the women across the river so they don't get wet. In this case she's carrying a child. It was a way of consolidating the family idea with the idea of the illegal alien." Jiménez dedicated the work to his father who had always said, "You know I was never an illegal alien, I just never had my papers straight."[9]

Jiménez went on to celebrate working-class heroes and the dignity of labor. *Sodbuster, San Isadora* is a farmer toiling behind a plow. *Steelworker* is a lithograph that shows the strength and character of the common laborer. Ordinary people come to life in Jiménez's artwork. He creates images of everyone just having a good time, as in *Honky Tonk* and *Fiesta Dancers*, which are at once familiar and funky.

Although many of his works now inhabit prestigious museums and elite New York galleries, as well as the homes of wealthy collectors, Luis Jiménez continues to mold images of American Indians, farmers, immigrants, and workers all engaged in action: just everyday people, plowing, herding cattle, forging rivers, and dancing.

Jiménez has also been an inspiration and mentor for young Chicano artists. His success in the world of fine art has led young artists to persevere in their dreams to become artists. One such artist is Jesús Bautista Moroles. Born in 1950 in Corpus Christi, Texas, Moroles became Jiménez's apprentice in 1979.

Moroles recalled that from his earliest childhood years in a public housing project in Dallas, Texas, he displayed artistic talent. His mother, a Latina born in Texas, and his father, a Mexican immigrant from Monterrey, encouraged Moroles by displaying his drawings and teaching him a variety of manual skills. Moroles refined his carpentry techniques by helping his father renovate their home when they moved to a new neighborhood. Moroles also spent many boyhood summers on the Texas coast with his uncle who was trained as a master mason in Mexico. Together, they worked on various construction jobs, including masonry work on a Gulf Coast seawall. This proved to have a lasting influence on Moroles' work.

After studying commercial art and enrolling in technical training courses, Moroles decided to go to college and study art. Even after serving four years in the Air Force, Moroles remained determined to study art and become a sculptor. He took drafting, electronics, math, and woodworking courses at North Texas State University (now the University of North Texas), graduating in 1978.

After graduation, Moroles began working as an apprentice to Jiménez. Moroles considers this apprenticeship to have been an important event in his artistic life. While their approaches to sculpture differ—Jiménez uses industrial materials to render realistic, figurative popular images, while Moroles works with natural material to create abstract images—the work of both artists reflects their Mexican heritage.

Following his apprenticeship, Moroles traveled to Italy to master the technique of carving marble. When he returned to

Texas he decided that granite would be the medium for his work. He had worked with granite back in his university days. He remembers, "I had a hammer and I had to hold on to it with both hands. I had to wear ear plugs, goggles, a mask for the dust, a scarf, and a hat. The clothing I was wearing over my own clothing was just caked with dust. I couldn't hear anything. I couldn't see anything." It was an experience that changed his life. "You're in there alone with that stone. You can only do it for about thirty minutes at a time. When I'd stop there would be about 30 people around me watching. It was so hard. It would take over me. And it barely showed what I'd done. I hadn't scratched the surface. It was really in control of me. I just fell in love with it."[10]

Moroles, as one of the few sculptors using granite, soon came to the conclusion that he needed more control over the process of creating his art. He established his own granite works, an "art factory" in Rockport on the southern Gulf Coast of Texas. The factory was definitely a family affair. His sister Susanna became his business manager, his brother worked with him, and his parents lived next door.

Moroles' 1988 sculpture *Granite Weaving* is a weaving of granite that alternates rough and polished surfaces, organic and geometric shapes, jagged and straight edges. It has the texture of woven stone and is part of the permanent collection of the National Museum of American Art in Washington, D.C. Moroles achieves the woven stone effect by slicing, chipping, grinding, and polishing pieces of granite. He uses power tools—drills, saws, and grinders—as well as traditional hand tools, such as chisels, picks, and hammers.

Moroles' 1993 installation *Tearing Granite: Thunder in the Stone*, presented at the University of North Texas, incorporates music and dance into his work. The original music includes the sounds of sawing, chipping, and carving granite mixed with percussion. Different parts of the installation are used as percussion instruments for the musicians and also form part of the dance routine. Moroles himself participates in the performance by actually "tearing" a piece of granite. This installation was shown later at the Institute of American Indian Art in Santa Fe where the performances were staged by American Indian artists.

Art critics often look for connections to ancient cultures from Mexico and Central America in Moroles's work. But the artist says his work is classical and that he wants it to be understood as truly "international." Perhaps so many people perceive cultural influences in Moroles's work because his classical training in art and his knowledge of cultural history makes his work a true synthesis of his personal history, knowledge, and experience.

The ceramist Michael Lucero is a good example of this international trend. He creates his art from clay, in a unique style that echoes his cultural roots as a Chicano while incorporating elements from other cultures. It has been said that Lucero was a multiculturalist before multiculturalism was cool. He has spent the better part of his career exploring materials and cultures not considered to be worthy of attention by art establishment gurus.

He was inspired during his time at the University of Seattle, where he earned a Master of Fine Arts degree. "I had funky teachers—female artists who identified with weaving and knitting, who used crafty techniques," says Lucero. Their example led Lucero to reject the conventional ceramics styles from Asia and study the pottery traditions of the Americas instead. Lucero's work is a cultural mixture of pre-Colombian figures, American Indian and African styles, and his own experiences—from childhood summers in New Mexico where he became fascinated with insects to his subsequent urban existence in New York. Fashioning clay heads decorated with fantastic dreamlike landscapes, turtles and moths, sculptures of beetles and frogs, pots strewn about with skeletons made from tiny bits of clay, Lucero is said to capture the "character of global culture." Sometimes he takes his formed and glazed ceramic pieces and combines them with garden statues, baby carriages, African carvings, and driftwood. His cement statue *Conquistador* is a Spanish soldier with a bright red teapot for a head. In 1997, a twenty-year retrospective show of Lucero's works toured major museums.

Two other successful artists are Amalia Mesa-Baines of California and Carmen Lomas Garza of Texas. Mesa-Baines combines the folk art traditions of altars made by Mexican women with installation art. She has emerged as an active spokeswoman for Chicana artists. For her installations, Mesa-Baines makes her own altar clothes and paper flowers and cuts her own paper (*papel picado*); she hires a carpenter to help her build the *nichos* and *retablo* boxes. Her work, which has been exhibited nationally and internationally, has a moving spiritual sensibility.

The work of Carmen Lomas Garza celebrates the commonplace everyday features of Chicano culture, as in her 1987 *El Milagro*. She has been compared to the great Mexican artist Frida Kahlo, who combined magical and powerful images of traditional Mexico interwoven with political and personal messages. In a 1997 interview, Lomas Garza said that she hopes people "who are not Mexican American or Latino can see my artwork and get a better idea of who we are as Mexican Americans, and also see similarities from their own cultures."[11]

Artist Carmen Lomas Garza at her studio sitting by her painting **Una Tarde**

Carmen Lomas Garza

Born 1948, Kingsville, Texas

Garza's family came to the United States to escape the hardships of the Mexican revolution during the early 1900s. At a very early age, she wanted to pursue her dream of becoming an artist. She taught herself to draw by practicing every day. She drew whatever was in front of her that would stay still for a few minutes. She received her master of arts degree from San Francisco State University. Much of Garza's work focuses on the traditions and daily activities in Mexican-American culture. Her paintings have been exhibited across the United States and other countries in galleries and museums. Her work is in both private and public collections, including the Hirshhorn Museum and Sculpture Garden in Washington, D.C.

As an activist in the Chicano movement, Carmen Lomas Garza sees her art as a conscious statement of her own experiences growing up in Texas. At age thirteen, she realized she wanted to become an artist. A major influence was her mother, who created *loteria tablos*, which resemble illustrated bingo cards. She drew little figures, using pen and ink and watercolors. Lomas Garza took her first art classes in high school and then completed her education at San Francisco State University.

She decided to make her art simple, straightforward, and rooted in her Chicana experience. "Very deliberately, after having learned all the principles of art and the Renaissance elements of art and all the academic stuff, I chose to drop some of those concerns and do my artwork as simple and as direct as possible," she explains. "I really wanted to be able to communicate. I felt that I could not afford to lose my Mexican American audience."

Lomas Garza's colorful figures go about their daily business along with *curanderas* and beautiful intricate steel cutouts modeled after traditional *banderitas* (Mexican hand-crafted objects made of tissue paper). In one piece a *curandera* is trying to cure a teenage girl of rebelliousness. The girl is the artist's sister, and Lomas Garza says it worked! Some of her subjects are special occasions, like weddings, dances, and healing rituals. These works are familiar but with a definite Chicano flavor that invites the viewer right into the homes and streets of barrio life.

Lomas Garza's work has been included in several shows organized by major museums in order to showcase Latino art. One of the first, "Hispanic Art in the United States," toured nationally in 1987–1988. The traveling exhibit was "quite an eye-opener," said Lomas Garza. "I could tell when a museum truly wanted to promote the work, or was doing it for political and financial reasons."

Her own deep political commitment is reflected in her reaction to another major show that featured Chicano art produced during two decades of struggle for equal rights. Entitled "C.A.R.A, Chicano Art: Resistance and Affirmation 1965–1985," the exhibit opened in 1990. "When it first opened and I started to walk through it," she said, "I just started crying because it brought back so many memories of the Chicano movement, of the early days, of all the turmoil that we went through, all the criticism, the danger, the risk, the sacrifice that we had to make as artists in order to bring about civil rights for the Mexican American population."

As a famous Latina artist in the United States, Carmen Lomas Garza feels a need for Chicano artists to connect with Mexican artists who share the same roots and the same border. "The mainstream of art in Mexico has always been following New York," she said. "Chicanos have not been following New York or Paris." According to Lomas Garza, a major difference between Chicano and Mexican artists lies in their respective attitudes toward Mexican folk art. "In Mexico the folk art is folk art; it's not respected like fine art," she noted. "But here the Chicanos have always revered the folk art and we've incorporated it in our artwork." Lomas Garza believes the reason for this attitude is based in class differences. "Part of it has to do with the fact that some of us who have migrated here from Mexico come from the poorer classes, the working classes, the farmworkers who are the Indians or the mestizos and not the European, white Mexican." She remembers the early days of the Chicano movement, when the Mexicans regarded Chicanos as "traitors," "outcasts" and "gringos." "We were neither here nor there. There was always a little bit of a rejection," she pointed out.

Since then, a new spirit of shared cultural values that crosses the border has emerged. "The Mexicans are becoming much more interested now in Chicanos," Lomas Garza observed. "The Mexicanos are finally realizing: We're kind of important, we're carving the way through. And more and more Mexico is having a much tighter relationship with the United States. It's becoming much more intertwined because of the economy, because of the population, the numbers. The United States is having to deal with Mexico."

Border Art

Many would agree with Lomas Garza, especially judging by the explosion of highly imaginative artworks and performances taking place in the cities and towns along the 2,067-mile (3,326-kilometer) U.S.–Mexico border or in the interior of either country. One of many examples of cross-border art is the 1997 Chicago mural *Hands in Solidarity—Hands of Freedom*. It was painted on the exterior wall of the Electrical Workers Union UE District 11 Hall by three young muralists from the world-famous Chicago Public Art Group and the famous muralist Daniel Manrique of the neighborhood-based Tepito Arte Aca group from Mexico City's slums. Sponsored by the UE and Mexico's independent Authentic Workers Front (FAT), it shows two symbolic hands holding a lightning bolt, plus an additional pair of hands clasped together, to illustrate the freedom and strength of working people uniting across borders in international solidarity. The Chicago mural completed an international effort that included a mural by a U.S. artist at the FAT headquarters in Mexico City.

The border's significance as a historical and social reality is the focus of many Chicano artists who dramatize the border culture in their works. The politics of migration and illegal immigrants has long been a hot issue, with television images of helicopters and dogs hunting down immigrants and depicting the border as a veritable war zone. In his performance art and theater works, Guillermo Gómez Peña often describes the border as "a multiple metaphor of death, encounter, fortune, insanity, and transmutation."

In the early 1980s, a group of artists from Mexico and the United States formed the San Diego-based Border Arts Workshop to dramatize the human side of the story and promote greater understanding of the lives of migrants in today's world. The artists worked collectively, creating street theater, public performances, installations, music, video, and storytelling, and always inviting their audiences to participate. They took their show on the road, hitting countless border towns and crossing spots along the border as well as cities with large migrant populations like San Francisco and border cities to the north and east, like Buffalo, New York, near the U.S.–Canada border. They became quite controversial because of their portrayals of police brutality and pesticide use, migrants being run down by cars on freeways, and insensitive if not stupid *migra* agents. Their Café Urgente was fast-paced living theater that involved and delighted audiences everywhere.

The Border Arts Workshop quickly caught the attention of the art world. It was invited to perform in galleries in New York, at museums across the country, and even in Europe. Border Arts Workshop became the rage in the late 1980s. But the artists never forgot their audience and continued to perform in migrant camps and in schools, as well as in towns on both sides of the border, bringing audiences their message of respect and understanding of the migrant experience.

The migrant experience is, of course, not unique to Chicanos, but the geographical closeness of Mexico and the flow of families back and forth across the Río Grande is key to understanding Chicano art and artists. As one artist explains, "As a first-generation American, I am forever marked by migration and loss, forever marked by the specter of the border that separates me from my history and my original land."[12]

Puerto Ricans: From *Santos* to Avant-Garde

The story of Puerto Rican art is a story of a lasting culture and yet radical change. In order to understand this art, we must look into the experiences of the people and how this beautiful mountainous Caribbean island has undergone so many changes at the hands of foreigners.

Since the first encounter with the Spanish in 1492, the island has been shaped by a legacy of military conquest and occupation. The original inhabitants were the Arawak, a highly intelligent people who shortly after the Spanish invasion suffered epidemics and disease that virtually erased all traces of their civilization. The Spanish settlers intermarried with the survivors, who were then joined by thousands of African slaves brought to the island to work on the sugarcane plantations. The Africans and their cultures added their traditions of worship and art that would become a lasting influence in Puerto Rican culture.

The Arawak Taino Indians were part of a large civilization that established itself in many islands of the Caribbean. Nowhere was their culture more developed than in Puerto Rico, a place they called *Boriquen* (Land of the Noble Lord). The Taino crafted beautiful objects called *cemi*. Made of carved wood and stone, the *cemi* were thought to have spiritual powers. Today there is a renewed appreciation for the Taino culture, and many Puerto Rican artists yearn to reclaim the Taino heritage.

The arrival of the Spanish brought death and slavery, and the surviving Taino traditions quickly became absorbed into the reigning European culture. During the four hundred years of Spanish rule, the island was transformed into a major trading port and hub for the loot from the conquest of Mexico on its way back to Spain. As part of the Spanish Empire, Puerto Rico played a key role in the flow of goods and people throughout the region. Its sugar and rum were highly valued, attracting merchant ships and pirate ships to the island's inlets and harbors. As Puerto Rico became linked with other Latin American colonies and the world, Puerto Ricans became very cosmopolitan, at least among the ruling classes, and developed close ties to Europe and Latin America.

When Latin America's colonies revolted against Spain in the early 1800s, Puerto Rico joined the fight, but its attempts to throw off colonial rule proved unsuccessful. Many of the island's freedom fighters were killed or were forced into exile. Several fled to the United States, establishing the first Puerto Rican communities in New York and Florida.

During the rest of the 1800s, the power of the Spanish Empire was waning but Spain clung to its two prized possessions

in the Caribbean—Puerto Rico and Cuba. The uprisings continued, and, under this pressure, slavery was abolished in 1873.
Working together, Puerto Ricans and Cubans continued their
struggle for independence.

In 1897, Spain granted limited independence to Puerto
Rico—but not to Cuba, whose massive slave uprisings made it
too risky. Within months, the United States invaded both islands
and, in the Treaty of Paris, Spain ceded Puerto Rico to the
United States. Yet no Puerto Rican leaders were part of this deal.
However, the treaty granted Cuba independence, mainly because
the Cuban freedom fighters and their political spokesmen were
still so insistent on independence and Cuba was thought to be
too difficult to govern.

Meanwhile, after shelling the capital city of San Juan, U.S.
troops occupied Puerto Rico and kept it under military rule for
two years until a governor was appointed by the U.S. president.
The hopes and aspirations for Puerto Rican independence were
dashed—one master had been replaced by another.

While the island was officially called "unincorporated territory," Puerto Rico was treated like a U.S. colony. As a result, the
island experienced rapid economic change when large U.S. sugar
companies bought up land on the island. The farming communities that had been the island's source of food and rural way of life
started to disappear. Working for the sugar companies became the
only means of survival for many people. Yet they soon found that
they could not provide for their families with the ridiculously low
wages paid by the companies. They left the land in droves, mov-

ing to the cities in search of work and a better life. But the over-crowded cities could not provide jobs or decent housing.

Public education was available but instruction was carried out in English. As a result, many young Puerto Ricans left school. When Puerto Ricans were declared citizens in 1917, some 18,000 joined the U.S. Armed Forces and went off to fight in World War I (1914–1918). An exodus from the island, encouraged by U.S. mainland employers offering jobs, started in earnest in the 1920s. By 1926, more than 150,000 Puerto Rican immigrants had arrived in the Puerto Rican barrio of New York City. During the Great Depression of the 1930s, the exodus became a massive movement north to escape the epidemic of poverty that gripped the island.

Gone forever was the peaceful way of life of farmers who, for generations, had tended their small plots. Waves of desperate emigrants crowded boats, and later planes to arrive in the "promised land" of New York. The new arrivals, denied basic civil rights in their native land, came to the mainland in search of a better life. Those who stayed behind did not abandon the struggle for national independence.

Luis Muñoz Marín, before he became governor of Puerto Rico, once described the oppression and suffering of the Puerto Rican people under U.S. rule as follows:

> *The American flag found Puerto Rico penniless and content. It now flies over a prosperous factory worked by slaves who have lost their land and may soon lose their guitars and their songs. In the*

old days most Puerto Rican peasants owned a few pigs and chick-
ens, maybe a horse or a cow, some goats, and in some way had a
patch of soil. . . . while there are many more schools for their hun-
gry children and many more roads for their bare feet, their destiny
is decidedly narrower now. [1]

Pressing for change, Muñoz Marín helped found a pro-independence political party that made him the first elected governor
of the island in 1948. But he soon abandoned the cause of independence and other politicians who championed independence
were murdered and jailed. In 1952, Puerto Rico became a commonwealth of the United States, remaining a U.S. territory without its own independent government.

From 1946 to 1964, in spite of a mighty effort to improve
conditions on the island through the creation of manufacturing
plants and jobs, more than one million people left the island for
the mainland. Starting in the mid-1960s, an old type of migration, "the revolving door," became more common—going back
and forth between the mainland and the island. By 1980, almost
half of all Puerto Ricans lived inside the United States, but many
spent part of the time on the island.

New Puerto Rican arrivals in the United States, like those
before them, were met with racism and treated like African-Americans. Consequently, the civil rights movement of the 1960s
ignited a movement for equal rights among Puerto Ricans both
on and off the island. In the U.S. cities of the North and Midwest, the Young Lords, initially a street gang allied with high
school and college students, gained national attention as

spokespersons for a new generation. They were pro-independence and called for equal civil rights, equal rights for women, and an improvement in the living conditions of the barrios. They also called for "a true education of our Afro-Indio culture and Spanish language."

During this time, just as happened with the Chicanos, an interest in identity and roots developed. This led to a search for cultural roots in the Taino culture, the colonial traditions, and the bicultural mainland experience in the streets of New York, Chicago, and other cities.

Santeros, Then and Now

The meaning of the mixed heritage of pre-Colombian, Spanish, and African cultures was explored by a new generation of artists, and a new respect for the artistic traditions of the island drew their eyes to the art of the *santeros*, the carvers of holy images. Fashioned of clay, stone, gold, and wood, figures of saints and other religious figures are part of a centuries-old tradition, dating back to the 1500s.

Like the *santero* art of the Southwest, the carving of sacred Christian images began under Spanish rule, but with a twist. These images were used in family homes and community rituals. They were treated like members of the family, dressed and cared for, and thought to grant favors and protection. Belief in the power of *santos* to intercede between people and the forces of heaven is part of the spiritual side of life that is so important to Puerto Ricans. They share some of their beliefs and practices with the Afro-Cuban religion of Santería, but the miraculous and spiritual side of the supernatural is much more pronounced in Puerto Rican culture. It is thought that the ancient Taino tradition of carving *cemí* figures might have inspired the making and worship of *santos*.

The most continuous tradition of *santero* carving dates from the mid-1700s. The earliest *santos* emerged in Puerto Rico's central mountainous region. The carving of saints' images may have been born of geographic and economic necessity. The remote locations of these villages made it difficult to reach churches, which gave rise to home-based worship. It is also true that statues produced by local carvers were cheaper than European imports. Also, the beautiful hand-carved figures may have been the result of a preference for local favorite saints that reflected worship unique to Puerto Rico.

Antique *santos* were carved of native woods, including cedar, oak, and laurel. Then, like their New Mexican counterparts, they were covered with gesso (a type of sealant) and painted with oil- or vegetable-based paint. Many of the oldest *santos* have layers of paint, each coat signifying a favor granted. Many of the antique *santos* show the effects of being placed near candles, their surfaces exposing layers of different paints with bubbling heat cracks.

Traditionally, *santos* are displayed on small altars in homes. Lovingly cared for, they are often dressed and decorated with flowers and offerings. Families would gather at home altars to express devotion, ask for favors, and sing and pray.

Favorite *santos* include statues of the three kings, the archangels, and the Virgin Mary. They can often be identified by their clothing or by the objects they hold. Saint Anthony, for

Myrna Báez

El Tocador

1985

Acrylic on canvas

44 × 62 in.

(112 x 157 cm)

Jean-Michel Basquiat

Part Wolf

1982

Acrylic, oil stick, paper collage on canvas

74 ✕ 96 in.

(188 ✕ 244 cm)

Juan Sánchez
Confused Paradice
Oil, mixed media on wood
78 ✕ 66 in.
(198 ✕ 168 cm)

Juan Sánchez

Mixed Statement, *1984*

Oil, mixed media·on canvas
54 ✕ 96 in. (137 ✕ 244 cm)

Carlos Alfonzo

Dibujo y transfiguro (I Draw and Transfigure), 1976

Ink and gouache on paper

35 1/2 ✕ 32 in. (90 ✕ 81 cm)

Maria Brito
A Theory on the
Annihilation of
Dreams
1987
Mixed media
95 1/2 ✕ 61 ✕ 85 in.
(243 ✕ 155 ✕ 216 cm)

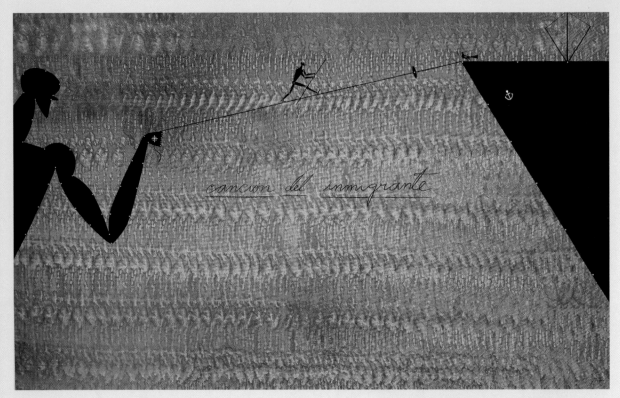

José Bedia

Immigrant Song (Cancion del Immigrante), 1994

Acrylic on canvas

42 × 70 in. (107 × 178 cm)

Maria Brito

Altar

1987

Mixed media

42 × 40 × 11 1/4 in.

(107 × 102 × 29 cm)

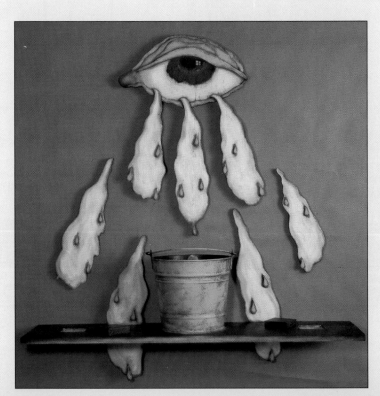

Luis Cruz Azaceta

Self-Portrait: Feeling the City of Lights on in My Head

1983

Acrylic on canvas

66 × 60 in. (168 × 152 cm)

Juan Boza

Abakua #6, 1986

Intaglio print with Bob Blackburn

35 × 24 in. (91 × 61 cm)

example, is always shown in a brown robe, carrying the baby Jesus or a book. Rafael, the archangel, clutches his miraculous fish. The three kings are mounted on their horses—the African king always rides the white horse.

Contemporary *santos* can be seen in restaurants and churches, as well as in galleries and museums. In Puerto Rico, the Museo del Arte de Ponce offers a biennial exhibit of contemporary *santos*, helping to increase people's appreciation of this art form. In New York, the Museo del Barrio has a large collection of antique and modern *santos* that were put on display in 1997. Noted one prominent art critic: "Among the most moving works in the great tradition of devotional art in the Americas are either carved or painted wooden holy images from the Caribbean known as santos."[2]

Lares Group **San Antonio y el Nino (Saint Anthony and Christ Child)**

Artists' Concern for Social Justice

Another tradition in the arts that Puerto Rican artists were quick to build on was the use of paintings, graphics, and ceramics to make political statements or carry messages of social concern.

Many artists in the 1950s and 1960s were disturbed by the continued colonial political status of Puerto Rico.

The tradition of political art on the island goes back to Francisco Oller, a nineteenth-century painter who believed that art has a "political, social and religious mission." His masterpiece, *El Velorio*, depicts a wake for an infant, with both Christian and African symbols of mourning. Oller helped found art schools, and his legacy inspired growing numbers of artists in the 1950s.

At that time, the island government's Division of Community Education sponsored graphic arts workshops that began making posters. The posters and prints soon gained a world repu-

Francisco Oller **El Velorio** *1893*

tation for their excellence. Silk screens and wood and linoleum cuts were used to create prints that contained political commentaries as well as public service messages. Many were for public health and education. Some simply celebrated Puerto Rico's culture in a patriotic way.

The graphic arts movement produced striking prints that caught the attention of art critics and collectors around the globe. Its workshops also lured a generation of artists back to the island, people like Rafael Tufiño (from Mexico), Carlos R. Rivera, and Julio Rosario del Valle. The returning artists became leaders of the new Puerto Rican art movement and brought it international acclaim.

Lorenzo Homar is considered the father of the poster movement. As one of the original poster artists and a founding member of Puerto Rico's famed *Taller Gráfico* (Graphics Workshop), he developed an exacting technique that resulted in beautifully detailed prints and set a high standard for young artists. His famous woodcut *El Maestro* (The Teacher) commemorates Pedro Albizu Campos, a persecuted leader of the Puerto Rican independence movement who spent most of his life in jail.

As the director of the *Taller Gráfico* at the Institute of Puerto Rican Culture, Homar created a rich artistic legacy of his own while training a new crop of younger artists. Two of these exceptionally talented artists, Antonio Martorell and Myrna Báez, became famous both on the island and in New York. Like their mentor, these two artists combined their art with their political commitment to social justice and Puerto Rican independence.

> ## *Lorenzo Homar*
> ### Born 1913, Puerta de Tierra, Puerto Rico
>
> Homar was born in Puerto Rico, but grew up in New York City.
> He attended the Brooklyn Museum Art School and studied metal-
> work at Cartier's, a company that designs and manufactures
> jewelry and **objets d'art**. In 1950, he returned to Puerto Rico,
> where he was active in the graphic arts and one of the founders
> of the Puerto Rican Arts Center. He received a Guggenheim Fel-
> lowship in 1957. His lithographs, posters, and paintings hang in
> New York's Museum of Modern Art and the Library of Congress.
> Homar was one of the first artists in Puerto Rico to recognize the
> potential of the poster as an affordable art form.

Widely recognized as a painter and a graphic artist, Myrna Báez takes her role as a socially responsible artist very seriously. She recalls her years at the *Taller Gráfico*, saying, "Artists then were still committed to art and society. Today's commitment is to the art [market] . . . that changes the kind of art that is produced." As an educator, a successful artist, and a supporter of Puerto Rican independence, she is a role model for emerging women artists. She is renowned for her pioneering techniques in colorful prints that capture breathtaking tropical landscapes and ocean-reflected light. Her landscapes sometimes show the encroachment of the tourism industry's "maracas and concrete" on Puerto Rico's peaceful countryside.

Báez also captures the beauty of Puerto Rican customs and

traditions. Her love of the island and its people comes in part from her belief that each person is formed by their native landscape— that it exists inside you and you take it wherever you go. In her paintings, Báez often portrays the Puerto Rican upper classes in a comic way that mocks their pretentious imitations of Anglo-European customs and society.

Myrna Báez is known for her depictions of Puerto Rican life and the island's landscapes.

This type of social criticism is also seen in the work of Antonio Martorell, another political activist and member of the *Taller Gráfico*. Before venturing into the art world, Martorell received a degree in diplomacy from Georgetown University in Washington, D.C. When he returned to Puerto Rico, he trained as an apprentice under the Spanish painter Martin-Caro and studied graphic art. In the late 1960s, Martorell founded his own independent workshop on the island—the *Taller Alacrán*. He produced political posters, commercial art, and various works that showcased his biting political wit. In his giant-sized playing cards *Barajas Alacrán* series, the joker is then-U.S. president Lyndon B. Johnson dressed as a Puerto Rican cowboy.

Martorell has applied his talents to painting, illustration, set design, and acting. His dark sense of humor is evident throughout his work. His 1980 interactive show, "White Christmas," took a jab at the upper classes' "wannabe" imitation of Anglo culture and a pathetic real event. It featured typical Puerto Rican tourist scenes covered with snow on a series of postcards. He invited his audience to wear winter clothes to the show, having in mind the wealthy classes' mania for "White Christmas" debutante balls during the 1960s. He also poked fun at an absurd but real event that took place in 1952, the year Puerto Rico became a commonwealth of the United States, when the mayor of San Juan arranged to fly a planeload of snow to the island for children to play in.

Because of his continued commitment to the cause of independence, Martorell's home was invaded and ransacked by agents from the Federal Bureau of Investigation (FBI). This harassment led to a demonstration by several hundred supporters at the opening of his show "Blows." Turning his attention to multimedia installation, Martorell created a spectacular array of colorful woodcuts—a kind of Puerto Rican Garden of Eden populated by mythical figures and seen through the bars of a traditional colonial fence.

Martorell was not the only Puerto Rican artist to be hassled by the authorities for his political convictions. In 1980, Elizam Escobar, who had come to New York in the 1960s to study art and work at the Museo del Barrio, was convicted of seditious conspiracy and sentenced to sixty-eight years in prison. Behind bars, he continued creating powerful paintings, such as *Perfiles en un Album* (*Profiles in an Album*). The small painting shows the faces of two lovers looking at each other, across the spine of a photograph album meant to symbolize a prison bar. In September

1999, Escobar was released from jail under a presidential order of conditional amnesty for fifteen Puerto Rican political prisoners. He and the other released prisoners were given a rousing welcome in San Juan, Puerto Rico.

Avant-Garde in New York

Several gifted and politically committed Puerto Rican artists have come from the streets of New York City. Through their political activity and their creative work, they strive to tell the story of the *Nuyorican* experience. (A Nuyorican is a New Yorker of Puerto Rican descent.) Their bold work has enlivened the art scene in the city known as the world's art capital. They and others have helped make possible the creation of such world-class art museums as the Museo del Barrio in Manhattan and the Bronx Museum of the Arts, both of which retain close links with the local Puerto Rican and Latino communities. Starting in the 1970s, it became common for Nuyorican painters and sculptors to interact with poets and dramatists giving readings of their work at the Nuyorican Poets Café founded by poet Miguel Algarín on Manhattan's Lower East Side. This added to the city's cultural renaissance then taking place.

Juan Sánchez is one of these artists. The son of Afro–Puerto Rican parents, he has achieved critical acclaim from the fancy New York art world without ever abandoning his roots on the streets of Brooklyn. In carrying on the Puerto Rican tradition of protest and politics through art, he states: "My art is inspired by the fact that even though the empire tries to buy the truth, the Puerto Rican people resist. They never allowed imperial powers

Since the early 1980s, Juan Sánchez has combined his artistic skills with political activism in his work.

to bury their island, their culture, their history, their lives."

Sánchez draws on the cultural threads of his heritage: Afro-Cuban religions and healing rituals, ancient Taino symbols, Christian saints, and graffiti. He combines these elements with the politics of resistance to challenge mass-media stereotypes. He shows family life and barrios as a source of strength and pride.

Growing up, Sánchez often helped his father carve decorative home altars for friends and neighbors. During high school, his teachers quickly recognized his talent and encouraged him to pursue his studies at Cooper Union in Manhattan. As a member of the *Taller Boricua*, he met another young artist, who was also a native Nuyorican, Jorge Soto. A self-taught artist, Soto's canvases reflect his appreciation of Taino and African aesthetics. His line-drawing technique and use of tropical foliage have a distinctive character.

About this time, Sánchez became politically active. He attended a few meetings of the Young Lords Party and went on to become active in protesting South Africa's apartheid and human rights violations. At the same time, he worked to bring attention to the work of minority artists.

Sánchez's academic studies reflect the wide range of his talent and interests. At Cooper Union, and later at Rutgers University, Sánchez studied graphic design, photography, painting, and art history. He credits this formal education with giving him the opportunity to develop his own style and sense of purpose.

In 1985, Juan Sánchez summed up his credo: "Political art is a medium used as a weapon to hopefully recapture or regain the positive energy of celebration—to regain the goodness of humanity." His well-known images of flag-draped figures, fallen heroes of the independence movement, the Statue of Liberty covered with a Puerto Rican flag, bloody handprints, fragments of dollar bills, and images of violence and pain are accompanied by representations of family love and spiritual faith.

Altars, saints, African deities, and mothers and children inhabit Sánchez's paintings, as do tropical plants, parade floats and pageants, and the walls and streets of city slums. The decaying urban landscape is his world. It inspires all his work and can be seen in his images of peeling walls layered with posters, handbills, graffiti, and grime.

Sánchez's art tells the story of the Puerto Rican people, who have survived in spite of racial prejudice and efforts to crush political dissent. Cultural and economic imperialism, poverty, and emigration are all themes in Sánchez's work. In telling this story, Sánchez's art celebrates the triumph of the Puerto Rican people's spirit. Sánchez has been awarded numerous fellowships, including ones from the Guggenheim Foundation and the National Endowment for the Arts. His works have toured major museums and galleries. He continues to live in Brooklyn, New York.

Two Puerto Rican artists who have had a major impact on

the New York art scene and influenced many younger artists are Rafael Ferrer and Rafael Montañez Ortiz. Each in his way has shaped a movement in the arts that changed the way people think about art.

Ortiz, who claims Puerto Rican, Chicano, and American Indian ancestry, was a leader of the "destruction in art movement" of the 1960s. He had started out in the late 1950s by making abstract expressionist style paintings, but soon began to explore destruction as a creative force. He stunned audiences by smashing pianos and sacrificing chickens. His mutilated mattresses and couches made powerful statements about violence in society. In protest of the war in Vietnam, he once turned loose a battalion of mice, each wearing a little soldier's "dog tag"—into a field of mousetraps. In 1973, Ortiz held what he called "Physio-Psycho-Alchemy" performances where he incorporated the dreams, inner visions, and emotions of the audience into his work.

Ortiz also uses his art to make statements about natural and supernatural forces and to question our perceptions of how the world should be. Later in his career, Ortiz embarked on a personal voyage of enlightenment. He studied ancient beliefs and ritual healing, animism, and ceremonial rites, even becoming a shaman, or priest. He has incorporated this knowledge into his performance art. One piece, performed in Milan, Italy, in 1992, is a ritual of listening to the voices of living trees.

As a teacher, a shaman, and an artist, Ortiz has maintained his ties to the community. He is a main founder of the famed Museo del Barrio in New York, which features work by Latino artists and serves as an educational and cultural center for the people of the barrio. Ortiz, who holds a doctoral degree from Columbia University, understands the tensions of living in two cultures. He is sensitive to the struggles of Latino artists to cross the barriers of prejudice, in the art world in particular. Of his own artwork, he says: "I never wanted to be folk Hispanic or folksy anybody, but have looked beyond my limitations. . . . This is why education is meaningful, so that art at the larger level of world problem solving becomes like any other profession."[3]

Rafael Ferrer, like Ortiz, uses his art to explore the unknown in original personal ways. He uses "process," or the act of creating, to get his audiences to think in new ways. As with Ortiz, Ferrer is a controversial figure, breaking the rules of the art establishment. He views these rules as having been made by the Anglo culture and, in Ferrer's eyes, rules are made to be broken.

As a teen, Ferrer left Puerto Rico by choice to attend a military school in Virginia. This experience left him convinced that he would never serve in the armed forces in any capacity. It also gave him a lifelong love of drums and drumming. He has spent various periods of his life playing in Latin clubs. It was in New York that he discovered the magic of Afro-Cuban rhythms, which he calls "the ability to bring out the tropical, primitive, emotional conditions of one's roots into the open and to rejoice in their messiness."

Ferrer began to study painting at the University of Puerto Rico. Going back and forth between the island and New York, Ferrer worked as a stage manager for a Broadway production, played music, acted, and, in his spare time, visited museums and galleries. He returned to the island to take a job editing film at the racetrack. Making instant replays, he learned how to use film in creative ways. He also met up with his lifelong friend Chafo. Together, they created a series of sculptures and paintings for a show at the University of Puerto Rico that created an instant scandal and public outcry for its portrayal of Puerto Rican culture and social taboos, such as interracial dating. The show was picketed.

On the island, Ferrer's art was considered too controversial. Taking up such taboos as sex and the subject of mixed racial heritage in a raw and aggressive way, Ferrer found himself at odds with the Puerto Rican art establishment. Art critics objected to his subject matter. They judged his conglomerations of old shoes, lumber, and junk-car parts as crude and sloppy, out of step with the proud Puerto Rican tradition of precise and careful technique. But of course that was precisely his idea, to throw off the conventional assumptions and challenge his audiences to look beyond the limits of the accepted ideas about what art should and should not be.

Shortly thereafter, Ferrer left for the mainland, and many younger artists followed his example. He settled in Philadelphia, teaching and experimenting with different materials, such as chain-link fences. He broke into the New York art scene by mounting a guerrilla-type operation. He and his students drove to New York and stealthily deposited piles of leaves, eighty-four bushels in all, at various galleries around Manhattan. The "Philadelphia Leaves" caper grabbed the attention of gallery owners and art reviewers. Soon Ferrer was invited to exhibit in museums and galleries in New York and Europe.

Ferrer created his pieces on the site of the shows, not in a studio. He used grease, straw, ice, and leaves to create sculptured spaces. *Ice* was notable for the fact that the sculpture, once finished, began its process of turning into water, shrinking and melting in front of the viewers. Playing by his own rules, Ferrer accepted a request for a piece at the Philadelphia Museum of Art. He decided he couldn't work within the confines of the museum itself so he decided to use the fountain at the entrance. Using his body to deflect the spray, he created a performance sculpture in the fountain. Other works by Ferrer have used neon signs, drums, wrecked boats, oars, wounded whales, and masks. In the 1980s, Ferrer returned to painting scenes of his native Puerto Rico.

Each in his own way—Sánchez, Ortiz, and Ferrer—has broken through the museum gates so long closed to Latinos. In the process, these three artists have created new definitions of art and new opportunities for Puerto Rican and other minority artists, who have in turn met with some success in the art world.

Younger Artists and Biculturalism

Three younger Puerto Rican artists exemplify the diversity of the modern art scene and the tension between island and mainland cultures. Mari Mater O'Neill left the island to live and study in New York for ten years, only to return to the island. Nick Quijano was born and spent his formative years in New York City, but then went to live on the island. Arnaldo Roche Rabell divides his time between Chicago and the island. All three have international reputations and their work has been exhibited widely in the United States, Europe, and Puerto Rico.

Born in San Juan in 1960, O'Neill studied art at Cooper Union in New York City. O'Neill has helped promote her country and fellow Puerto Rican artists by working as the editor and publisher of *El Cuarto del Quenepón*, a magazine that celebrates the history and art of Puerto Rico. Her own paintings are about herself and her world. She uses bright colors and images to show relationships, often between herself and her friends. Her imagination often takes off in punky hominess—tables laden with food, small comical figures from Puerto Rican folklore mixed with scenes of family and community life.

O'Neill is also concerned with the role of women in society. She is interested in relationships between women and men and the animal and spiritual sides of human nature. In one painting, the artist reclines on a bed, holding a skeleton of a shark's head. Her cat is curled on her shoulder, and a male figure tries to embrace her. In a miniature version of the scene, a kind of painting within a painting, there is a red-winged angel hovering over her. The artist said that "the shark, the food, the fallen angel . . . I associate food with sex through violence. That is why beds appear to be tables and I portray myself as the meal." Her paintings are full of images and figures—sometimes of her friend Myrna Báez, paying affectionate tribute to her fellow artist and role model.

New York-born Nick Quijano was raised in the Bronx but spent his summers in Puerto Rico with his cousins and other relatives. Young Quijano took full advantage of life in the "Big Apple." He recounts how, as a child, he visited museums, the United Nations, libraries, the planetarium, and movie theaters.

He also partook of barrio nightlife—several of his uncles played in nightclubs. His childhood experiences and those of his family inspire his paintings, telling the story of the simple pleasures and hardships of Puerto Rican immigrants and the strength of traditional values.

While he spent most of his time as a child in New York, his summers back on the island gave Quijano a host of treasured memories. He remembers being greeted at the airport by aunts, uncles, and flocks of cousins "with their dark curly hair, the smiles on their faces . . . the rush of hugs and kisses." It was on the island that he learned to ride a bicycle and fell in love for the first time. Of those days, Quijano recalls "the rice and beans, sun-drenched beaches, tropical fish, and beautiful bodies."

When he was fourteen, the family returned to the island. After high school, Quijano studied architecture at the University of Puerto Rico, but his true passion was painting. In 1972, when Nick was nineteen, his mother and her parents left the island for New York in order to get medical treatment for Nick's grandfather who was going blind. Nick's father followed them. While Nick began working on a degree from Columbia University, his mother took a job in a factory and his grandmother earned money as a cleaning woman.

In his paintings, Quijano portrays Puerto Rican customs and values, often through portraits of his family. In *First Love*, his grandmother is shown embracing a child amid lush tropical plants. *La Siesta* shows his maternal grandmother asleep on the couch of a New York apartment. The room is filled with family mementos, religious objects, devotional Virgin figurines, and angels. The coffee cup represents hospitality, the eyeglasses and notepad symbolize education, and the lottery tickets suggest the "American Dream." These objects are accompanied by the bright and colorful doilies common to Puerto Rican households (many women did needlework as a way to get extra income).

In 1988, Quijano began working in sculpture. Here too he uses household objects: shoe brushes, broken glass, a float from a toilet tank. Quijano finds beauty in the ordinary things that surround us.

Arnaldo Roche Rabell, born in 1955 in Santurce, Puerto Rico, spends part of the year in Chicago and part on the island. He has gained notoriety for his style of painting—body rubbings. He uses living bodies smeared with paint and rolled in canvas to create a painted image. His models are wrapped in paper or canvas that is covered in layers of paint. Roche Rabell traces the human form by scraping with spoons, spatulas, knife blades, and his hands to expose the colors underneath. Of this process, Roche Rabell states: "It is a ritualistic human interaction. More than a ritual, it is a growing process to discover myself. . . . I am touching bones, muscles, and fingernails. How close can I get? It's life that becomes a painting, sculpture that becomes a painting."

Roche Rabell believes in psychic powers, the spiritual dimension, the supernatural, and the power of dream states. He has done self-portraits with himself growing horns and dreamy landscapes of Chicago being overrun with a tropical Garden of Eden. His magical and supernatural visions appear in forms that are based in his shamanistic vision of healing and transformation. His often fantastic creatures appear as dreams and nightmares.

Arnaldo Roche Rabell

In other works, Roche Rabell depicts the tension that comes with the experience of living in two cultures. The work entitled *You Have to Dream in Blue* is about the racist attitudes that Puerto Ricans of African heritage must confront. Perhaps the dream states of his paintings are this artist's way of dealing with the realities of living in two worlds, an existence that all Puerto Ricans know whether they are in the cities of the United States or on their native island.

Puerto Rican artists have gained fame for some of their graffiti and mural work as well. Puerto Rican graffiti artists have a

Jean-Michel Basquiat standing by some of his work

long history, entering their second and third generations of accomplished work in areas like New York City. Brooklyn-born Jean-Michel Basquiat, who gained great fame in a short period and died of a drug overdose in 1988 at age twenty-seven, is still honored as a "master" in both graffiti street art circles and the wealthy world of art patrons and art buyers.

Born in 1960, Basquiat was the son of a Puerto Rican mother and a Haitian father. He eagerly read books and art history and taught himself anatomy. Basquiat left home as a teenager to live in Manhattan and supported himself by taking odd jobs and by playing in a band. In the late 1970s, Basquiat, using the name "SAMO," began to leave his mark on the streets of New York by writing statements such as "9 TO 5 CLONE" and "PLAYING ART WITH DADDY'S MONEY." While still a teenager, he transferred his graffiti talents to painting canvases, and earned almost instant stardom, as well as big bucks. In Basquiat's 1982 work *Per Capita*, we see an African-American person with a burning torch alongside per-capita-income figures from Alabama (the lowest) to Connecticut (the highest). "The black person is the protagonist in most of my paintings," Basquiat once said. "I realized I didn't see many paintings with black people in them."[4]

Puerto Rican murals now appear throughout the United States, most of them in New York, Newark, Chicago, and Philadelphia neighborhoods, schools, and colleges. Many Puerto Rican artists cooperate with other Latino, Latin American, African-American, and Anglo artists in the increasingly internationalist and multicultural mural movement.

cuatro

Cuban Americans: Searching for Freedom

Many Cubans left their island country for personal, political, and economic reasons, and came to the United States looking for freedom. They brought with them a set of traditions that express the rich diversity of cultures. African, Spanish, and indigenous elements combined in an astonishing tapestry of religion, politics, and customs originating in their Caribbean homeland.

Located only 90 miles (145 km) from Florida's shores, Cuba has sent many of its most talented sons and daughters to the United States, many fleeing the turmoil that has afflicted its history since the early 1800s when the political crises of Spanish colonial rule forced Cubans to seek refuge in the United States. This "coming to America" and the search for freedom by some Cubans continue to the present day.

The earlier, often harsh imposition of Spanish colonial rule on Cuba was caused in part by the constant struggle of the Cuban people for freedom. Slave uprisings, civil war, tyranny, corruption, conspiracy, piracy, and persecutions are the bloody hallmarks of Cuban history, often complicated by U.S. intervention.

The United States has long maintained a keen interest in Cuba. Successive U.S. governments viewed the island as a strategic asset because of its nearness and economic potential. In the decades leading up to the American Civil War (1861–1865), some Americans wished to annex Cuba to the United States as a slave-holding state in order to strengthen the South and protect its system of slavery. The continued illegal slave trade in Cuba during those times resulted from a booming sugar trade that depended for its profits on slave labor. Roughly one-half of all Cubans were slaves.

Cuba's struggle for freedom and independence from Spain was also a struggle for the abolition of slavery. It was a long and bloody fight. Leaders of slave revolts were tortured and killed. Over a ten-year period (1868–1878), more than 250,000 Cubans died—one-fourth of the island's inhabitants. The United States served as a safe harbor for some of these freedom fighters, as Cuban patriots continued their struggle from afar. Exiled poets in New York City designed and sewed the first Cuban national flag. One of the most famous Cuban American artists of the twentieth century—Ana Mendieta (1948-1986)—was a descendant of these exiles.

In 1895, the great poet and patriot, José Martí, living in exile in New York, proclaimed Cuban independence and declared war on Spain. This attempt led to Martí's death in battle upon his return to Cuba. It also unleashed a wave of terror by the Spanish, who were determined to crush any resistance to their rule. In spite of the ruthlessness of Spain's grip on the island, the uprisings continued and, in 1898, Spain reluctantly granted Cuba home rule as a means to peace. The Cuban freedom fighters, however, on the verge of achieving a smashing military victory, demanded complete independence.

Then, on February 15, 1898, the U.S. battleship *Maine* exploded while anchored in Havana harbor. The United States blamed Spain, although subsequent evidence indicated that the explosion was caused by U.S. negligence of safety regulations.

The United States used the blowing up of the *Maine* to justify a declaration of war on Spain. Invasion and military occupation of Cuba followed, and after four years of U.S. rule, the island was granted independence in 1902. This did not bring an end to U.S. intervention, however, as U.S. troops continued to invade and occupy the island over the next thirty years in order to bring about "stability." Cuban independence brought with it a series of vicious and corrupt political regimes, propped up by the United States, that ultimately led to the 1959 nationalist revolution led by Fidel Castro.

For centuries, the spirit of the Cuban people in music, poetry, and the arts has endured successive dictatorships, authoritarian regimes, and broken promises. It is this legacy that contemporary Cuban American artists express so powerfully in their work.

These artists bring us their extraordinary visions of a tropical paradise left behind. Their work expresses the pain of loss and separation from friends, family, and homeland. It also explores the power of Santería (an Afro-Cuban religion), a world of dreams and magic, and statements about life in the United States. As a group, they represent the diversity of Cuban culture, while maintaining common roots in that same culture. Their talents are increasingly being recognized but, like other Latino artists, they face prejudice and stereotypes from the conventional art world. This is only gradually changing, however, because of their excellent work and that of other Latinos and people of color.

Generations of Cuban American Artists

Cuban American artists, whether born in Cuba or on the mainland, all work and reside in the United States. Generally, it is useful to think of contemporary Cuban Americans in terms of when they arrived in the United States.

The first generation of Cubans came shortly after the Cuban Revolution of 1959 that brought Fidel Castro to power. The revolution heralded drastic changes in the economic and political system of the country, changes that challenged the huge profits of U.S. sugar companies and banks. When the U.S. government implemented an economic embargo banning all U.S. trade with Cuba and, then, severed diplomatic relations, the revolutionary government sought economic survival and diplomatic support from the Communist countries. Tiny Cuba soon became a major player in the Cold War between the United States and the Soviet Union. The Cuban Missile Crisis of 1962 brought the world to the brink of nuclear war, when the United States discovered that the Soviets were building missile sites on Cuba.

By isolating Cuba, successive U.S. governments have believed that the economic embargo banning U.S. exports to Cuba would weaken the nation's Communist ties and bring about democracy. What it has done instead, as Pope John Paul II pointed out in his 1998 visit to Cuba, is to prolong the suffering and hardship of the Cuban people and give the Castro regime more excuses to impose strict constraints on those citizens who wish to leave.

Many of the first wave of Cuban immigrants to the United States were political exiles—people who opposed Castro or wealthy individuals who stood to lose property and privilege in the new socialist Cuba. They received economic support, free English-language classes, and several other benefits from the U.S. government, making their transition to life in the United States much easier than it was for other immigrants.

Most of this first generation of Cubans settled in Miami, where a thriving Cuban community soon became a powerful and prosperous force. "Little Havana," the section of the city where many Cubans live, became a mecca for artists and musicians, as well as businessmen and exiles plotting the overthrow of Castro. Stores, shops, clubs, and restaurants offering Cuban fare sprouted up to meet the needs of a community that maintained strong ties to the island's cultural traditions. The community supported theater, music, concerts, literature, and the arts. Some of this first generation came as adults, some as small children, and some as young teens. Many came alone because their parents or relatives were not able to leave Cuba.

Over the years, this first generation of exiles has been joined by a steady flow of Cubans seeking "political asylum" and a better life in the United States. In the mid-1990s, many of these new arrivals crossed the stretch of sea between Cuba and Florida in risky makeshift rafts, earning them the nickname of *balseros* (rafters). Several others lost their lives in the process.

The largest single exodus from Cuba occurred in 1980, when the Cuban government allowed thousands of people to leave for the United States in a massive boatlift from the port of Mariel. Flotillas of boats set out from Miami to provide passage, and 120,000 Cubans arrived on Florida's shores. They are known as the "Marielitos," after the point of their departure.

Since 1959, more than a million Cubans have settled in New York, New Jersey, and other locations as well as Miami. During this time, many of their children have grown up in the United States. They retain only faded memories of Cuba. Others were born in the United States and never knew Cuba firsthand. The younger Cuban Americans have experienced exile secondhand, but it still haunts their search for identity. Unlike some of their parents, however, they do not dream of returning to the island.

Although many young artists did visit Cuba during a short-lived thaw in U.S.–Cuba relations in the 1970s, none chose to stay. Even so, most Cuban American artists' work expresses a deep attachment to the island. It is reflected in their paintings of landscapes, of hills and sea, of palm trees, of African figurines, and of the gods and goddesses of Santería. As noted scholar Wayne Smith observed, Cuban Americans are Cuban but they are a new breed that through their artistic creations speak of "the myths, the dreams, the spirit, the rich mixture of African and Spanish blood that is Cuba."[1]

At the same time, they reflect something new: the experience and pain of the exodus, yet the themes and sense of their new home, the United States. They are Cuban *and* American, keeping their cultural heritage and putting down roots in U.S. soil.

This "uprooted yet putting down roots" feeling is described by photographer Margarita Paz-Partlow as "fitting neither here nor there." Paz-Partlow was brought to the United States by her mother in 1957 at the age of ten. She remains grateful to her mother for having "the courage to leave behind everything that was familiar and dear to bring us to the United States." Her childhood memories, both "lovely and wrenching," stay with her. Believing that her adopted homeland has given her "the freedom to choose whom I would become," Paz-Partlow affirms that, "Ours is a vast chorus enriched by the infinite variety of its voices: each deserves to be heard in its own time, in its own place."

Artist Mario Petrirena, who came with his family in 1962, said his work is about himself—raised in the United States, a son of Cuban parents. His family's strong beliefs and love for their homeland "influenced me and became part of me." He feels these influences are like "nourishment to the body. . . . we know oranges give us vitamin C and keep us from getting colds, but we don't always see the oranges. I feel the same way about my Cuban background. . . . a very important part of me and my work. . . . [I have] a bicultural background."

Maria Brito, who came to the United States at age thirteen, echoed Petrirena's feelings. Her art too is very personal. "My Cuban heritage, my Catholic upbringing, being uprooted, are . . .

part of me and part of the work I do." Her mixed media sculpture titled *A Theory on the Annihilation of Dreams* is based, like much of her work, on memories and feelings of solitude. "When I am alone working, I search into my own self a lot. I go back to when I was a kid . . . a lot of things happen when you are a child that you don't tell about. I am grown up, and I am safer now to tell these things." Brito is also concerned with how fear and intolerance of differences and the need for sameness can lead to the destruction of individuality and its beauty.

The concern with personal experiences, traditional and ancient forms of worship, and the search for identity has never been more dramatically depicted than in the work of the celebrated Ana Mendieta (1948–1985). Perhaps the best-known Cuban American artist, she was the first Latina to win a Guggenheim Award. Her intensely personal odyssey began with her upper-class upbringing in Cuba. In 1961, she and her sister were sent to the United States as part of Operation Peter Pan, a project funded by the U.S. Central Intelligence Agency (CIA) to bring Cuban children to the United States in the aftermath of the pro-Communist revolution in Cuba. Their parents remained in Cuba. Ana and her sister arrived only to be placed in a camp for juvenile delinquents. They were then transferred to a series of foster homes in Iowa, where they grew to adulthood. Their mother eventually joined them in 1967.

Ana pursued her passion for art, studying at the University of Iowa. She undertook a spiritual journey into the sacred world of nature. She was fascinated with the powers of the four elements: earth, wind, water, and fire. She used her own body to create art, scorching signs of herself in body prints of ashes, writing herself into the ground. The earth was her palette, and her body a brush. Her materials were gunpowder, firecrackers, mud, sand, cloth, tree trunks or branches, blood, feathers, and paint. Using rituals and symbols from Santería, she staged performances and created sculptures. She made many statements about the sacred connection between woman and nature, between the spirit and the flesh.

In speaking of her work, Ana Mendieta once said, "It is a return to the mother source—I become an extension of nature. My art is grounded in the belief in One Universal Energy which runs through all life and matter, all space and time. My works are the irrigation veins of this universal fluid. There is earth in the beginning, there is no past to redeem. . . . there is above all, a search for origin."

Part of this search took Mendieta back to Cuba, where she attempted to recover her roots in a series of cave paintings and sculptures, using Taino writings and images to connect with the ancient past. During this visit, she reached out to young Cuban artists, showing them new ways to look at life and art. One of these artists was José Bedia, a young painter who was fascinated by African and pre-Colombian ritual forms. In his friendship with Ana Mendieta, Bedia discovered a kindred spirit. It stimulated ideas in him of perhaps going to the United States himself.

Leaving Bedia behind in Cuba, Ana Mendieta returned to New York, where she achieved increasing acclaim for her work. At the height of her career, she met a tragic death in 1985. Through her work though, she remains a beacon to other Latina artists and an inspiration to her fellow Cubans. In her life and her art, Ana speaks to the world—and to the experience of many people in the United States whose lives have been shaped by forced emigration, persecution, and loss. Her work is a tribute to the power of myth, belief, and the strength of the spirit.

Ana Mendieta always viewed art as a pathway to liberation. Her ritual staged performances, many of them available on video-tape, became part of a new kind of public art. They ask us to respect nature, women, and the spirit that binds all of us to the earth.

Another successful Cuban American artist is Luis Cruz Azaceta, who came to the United States in 1960 at the age of eighteen. The oldest son of an airplane mechanic, he joined the hundreds of people seeking to leave Cuba at that time. He spent three days and nights waiting in line at the U.S. Embassy in order to get a visa to come to the United States.

Azaceta settled in a growing Cuban community in Hoboken, New Jersey, where he found work in a trophy factory and began taking drawing classes at a local community center. He then enrolled at the School for Visual Arts in New York, working his way through school as a library clerk. His first exhibition featured paintings of the New York subway system. They presented graphic and violent scenes of city life, stabbings, mutilation, and muggings in subway cars set in dreamy cityscapes, a comment on life in the "urban jungle."

In his series of self-portraits, the artist appears as many differ-

Luis Cruz Azaceta

ent people. They are persons who, in Azaceta's mind, are ignored
or forgotten by a society that reduces people to numbers or face-
less victims. In this way, Azaceta uses his own portrait to speak
out about AIDS, racism, and immigration in a world that ignores
basic human dignity. He has portrayed himself as a cockroach,

Luis Cruz Azaceta
Born 1942, Havana, Cuba

Azaceta moved to New York in 1960, one year after the Cuban revolution. He started to draw and paint on his own in 1963, and graduated from the School of Visual Arts in New York in 1969. In response to the anxiety of urban life in New York City, he began to paint monstrous figures, automobile accidents, skeletal images, and scenes of urban violence using harsh colors, energetic forms, and grotesque, anguished figures. His recent work has concentrated on social issues; for example, he has expressed his concern with the AIDS crisis through images of figures in coffins set before fields of numbers representing body counts. He was awarded fellowships by the National Endowment for the Visual Arts in 1980 and 1985, and by John Simon Guggenheim Memorial Foundation in 1985. His works have been included in exhibits throughout the United States, including The Museum of Fine Arts in Houston, the Indianapolis Museum of Art, and The Museum of Modern Art in New York. He currently lives in New Orleans.

a dog, a gunman, a cocaine addict, a *balsero* (rafter), Mickey Mouse, a homeless person, and someone with AIDS. His figures are victims of violence (*Gunman*), political oppression (*No Exit*), and exile (*Aliens: Refugee Count*). Hostages, dictators, and victims are portrayed with the artist's face. A critic once observed that looking at these self-portraits is not like getting to know the artist at all, but is more like meeting someone on the Internet.

Luis Cruz Azaceta **Split Head** *1983*
Acrylic on canvas
95 × 62 in. (241 × 157 cm)

You never really know who is on the other end.

Much of Azaceta's work reveals his concern with the plight of Cuban refugees who attempt the dangerous ocean crossing in makeshift boats and rafts, often made of scraps of wood lashed together with ropes. A catalogue from a 1997 Azaceta show notes that in *Rafter Hell/Act I* and *Caught*, the rickety rafts "seem to be held together by sheer will and the desire for freedom. For the lucky few who reach American shores their dreams will be met with the growing resentment against immigrants."

Azaceta's *SOS Tanker II* shows a huge ship being signaled by a tiny desperate figure flailing his arms. This painting reflects the true accounts of hundreds of rafters who have been rescued by commercial ships. It asks that we think about the continuing ordeal of these refugees, a situation worsened by the policies of the U.S. government, which closed the doors to Cuban refugees in 1994.

Like his self-portraits, these works are not based on Azaceta's own personal experience. After all, he flew to New York on one of the very last commercial flights to the United States out of Havana in 1960 before the U.S. government prohibited such flights. Nonetheless, the issue of immigration has continued to concern Azaceta. In the 1990s, he began to use Polaroid camera photographs and collages. In *Ark*, photos of hubcaps, sharks, rafts, and a crouching figure (the artist) show the dangers facing those who attempt the crossing. In *Immigrant*, a food processor and a blender represent the "American Dream" of modern consumer gadgets with the mixing of cultures that all immigrants must face.

In explaining his work, Azaceta says: "Cuba gave me my values, my sense of humor, and sarcasm; in other words, a tragic-comic look at life. The United States gave me the opportunity to become an artist, the freedom to paint the realities, anxiety, and horrors of the urban environment. The human condition." Speaking in response to how his work is "Cuban," he says:

> *Sunny breezy days, beautiful beaches, palm trees, sounds of marching boots, sirens, starry nights, dictator's terror, fear, torture, executions, carnivals and graves—all moving together with laughter, screams, and joy to the rhythms of merengues and cha-cha toward an unmarked pit. My concern is with humanity. I want to confront the viewer with life and what we are doing to each other. And although we try to manicure reality and make it like Hollywood—it is actually very brutal. I present victims in my work; that is my theme: human cruelty. Through it I hope to awaken a sense of compassion.*

Marielitos, Santería, and Beyond

The Marielito refugees who arrived in the 1980 boatlift came as adults and brought with them the experience of life under twenty years of Communist rule. While this part of their experience is present in their art, the Marielito generation also brought strong beliefs in the Santería forms of worship, an Afro-Cuban religion. The decade of the 1980s saw an upsurge of Santería in the greater Miami area, as thousands of followers set up altars in their homes. Shrines and offerings can now be found in public parks, on street corners, and even in police stations where sacrificial rituals are performed to honor *Ochassi*, the hunter-trapper god.

Two outstanding Marielito artists whose work explores the symbols and beliefs of the practice of Santería are Juan Boza and Carlos Alfonzo, both of whom died relatively young. Boza (1942–1991), whose works include montages, painted panels, and magnificently elaborate altars, once said: "My work is a visual language of sign, color and images, with a metamorphosis that is implicit in man, water, plants, animals, and objects: life."

After graduating from the National Academy of San Alejandro in 1962, Boza worked at the Experimental Art Printmaking Workshop as a lithographer for nearly ten years. In the United States, he became involved with the Art Students League and the Lower Eastside Printshop.

As an artist, Boza worked in the ancestral traditions handed down through generations of his family. Boza's altars combine the ideas of magic, ritual, and the sacred divinities of the Afro-Cuban religions. As he once explained: "The divinities of the

Yoruba are the responsibility of three cultures forcefully torn away from their [African] environment and brought to the New World to be dispersed in North and South America and the Caribbean."

Using decorative fabrics, leaves, metals, and offerings of fruit and flowers, Boza created beautiful statements that are reverent and powerful. His altar to *Yemaya*, the goddess of the sea and protector of fishermen, is entwined in a blue veil of gauze—netting for the fish—but royally draped in the way the Virgin Mary is often dressed. Here she is the ocean mother of the Yoruba, the "Queen of the Black Atlantic." Boza's art combines the mysteries of Santería and the spirits associated with rocks, animals, trees and nature with the power and energy of Yoruba gods, as in installations like *Prophecy of the King* (Portrait of Shango/Santa Barbara), which is surrounded by rich red fabric and brightly colored leaves. For Boza, just as for African cultures, life and art and life and religion are one.

The work of another Marielito, Carlos Alfonzo (1950-1991), also incorporates Santería symbols but goes beyond the traditions and creates "new symbols." Carlos was only ten years old when the Cuban revolution triumphed. The revolution encouraged art training for everyone regardless of the ability to pay, and Alfonzo spent his youth painting, achieving almost instant fame inside Cuba. His prominence as a young artist allowed him to express forbidden topics, although some U.S. art critics later alleged that they were disguised to confuse the authorities. Alfonzo himself claimed he was always on the edge of what would be tolerated.

Carlos Alfonzo

Born 1950, Havana, Cuba • Died 1991, Miami, Florida

Alfonzo attended art school and taught art history at a prominent art institute in Havana before moving to the United States in 1980. Alfonzo was a well-known artist in Cuba, but restrictions were placed on the subject matter of artwork, and Alfonzo had been told by several younger painters that his work was on the edge of what was allowed by the authorities. His paintings often include images of the cross, which he uses to represent spiritual balance. In his painting, **Mad One Also Sleeps** (1986), he uses tears as a symbol of exile. He earned the Cintas Fellowship in the Visual Arts in 1983, and received a fellowship from the National Endowment for the Arts in Painting in 1984. His works have been exhibited throughout Cuba and have been a part of several group shows in the United States including Intar Gallery and Kouros Gallery in New York, and throughout the southern Florida region. Alfonzo died of an AIDS-related cerebral hemorrhage in 1991.

Arriving in Miami in 1980 at the age of thirty, Alfonzo found the adjustment much more difficult than he had anticipated. He did not paint for a year. When he resumed painting, the pain of exile and learning that he was HIV positive became a central theme in his work. "My paintings have to do with my personal drama," he said. Shortly before his death in 1991, Alfonzo set out to paint his own epitaph: white blood cells, daggers, floating halos, crosses, and a mournful praying figure.

Alfonzo's works, exhibited in leading museums and including a commissioned mural, do not dwell on an idealized lost Cuban paradise. His pain was quite different, caused in part by the intolerance for homosexuality and people afflicted by AIDS inside Cuba. He was honored in "Triumph of the Spirit," a national touring retrospective show in 1997–1998 that featured many of his finest paintings.

Among the post-Marielito arrivals to gain attention is Ana Mendieta's Cuban friend José Bedia, who came to the United States in 1992. In a way, Bedia uses the common themes and concerns of the exiles who preceded him. But he also brings his personal experiences of growing up inside socialist Cuba and the strong respect he developed there for traditional cultures.

A child of the Cuban revolution, Bedia was born in 1959. In school he studied art but annoyed his teachers by making comic-book-style drawings based on his favorite comic book, *The Last of the Mohicans*. His drawing style, his interest in indigenous Caribbean and Ameri-

José Bedia

can Indian cultures, and his storytelling through pictures remain dominant in Bedia's approach to life and art. In one drawing, five little foxes are seated in a classroom, raising their paws enthusiastically to the teacher—except for one who dejectedly looks down. The accompanying text states "he'll never learn that."

This drawing reflects the artist's own frustration in school, which was turned around by a teacher who saw his talent. The teacher "saw me totally frustrated by learning academics, so he showed me another way. He showed me the connection between Cuban and African art." Young Bedia continued to develop his artistic skills in the art schools of Havana, but he found most of his instructors did not support his wish to explore the spiritual roots of Cuban culture. His teachers he remembers were "Soviet and very influenced by that style."

Just before he came to the United States in 1985 as a visiting young artist at State University of New York at Old Westbury, Bedia became a member of *Palo Monte*, a Congo-based religion that is popular in Cuba much as the Yoruba-based Santería is. Some of these spiritual beliefs can be seen in his work. Animals have supernatural qualities and can change into human forms. For example, deer are thought to be clairvoyant through their hooves, and they appear in his work amid traffic jams and overpasses, communicating the spirit world to the scenes of modern city life.

Bedia is interested in the folklore and rituals of the indigenous peoples that originally populated the Americas. Much of his work shows ceremonies and mythical stories from these cultures. In following a traditional religion, Bedia says he is trying to recover "my culture" and to establish a connection with the traditional teachings about the forces of nature.

Bedia's installation commemorating the "discovery of the New World" is a classroom. The blackboard is covered with the repeated phrase "*Viva el quinto centenario*" (hooray for the five hundredth centennial), written over and over like a bad student's punishment. In the background, a tree has been cut down by stacks of books. The student desks are covered with ceremonial herbs. This work honors the traditional ways of learning and wisdom and is a put-down of the Western custom of learning from books.

Having studied many traditional cultures, Bedia lives by surrounding himself with masks, carvings, drums, and beadwork from the Americas, Africa, and Asia. He believes in learning from different cultures. At the same time, his experience as an exile has meant trying "to reinvent my own country [and] conserve my own tradition."[2] In one of his paintings, a man is carrying his home and his family on his back as he steps from one clump of land to the next. Another shows a man astride a body of water with cars and buildings on each side. He is carrying a pouch filled with art supplies—below this figure is the artist's statement (and the title of the work), *If there is no sun in my own land, I'll jump to the other side*.

Here in the United States, Bedia has received recognition for his exceptional artistic talent and inventiveness. He often makes artistic use of found materials from alleys and streets. His paintings command unbelievably high prices, and his subject matter is unusual. It includes animals, insects, and birds, often in the style

José Bedia **Segundo Encuentro** *1992*

of hieroglyphics or cave paintings. In a world of high technology and "post-modern" problems, Bedia stands out for his fascination with Sioux drawings and other ancient ways.

While many Chicano, Puerto Rican, and other Latino artists feel perfectly free to extend their reach to revolutionary Cuba, most Cuban American artists do not. Indeed, within their own community their quest for freedom is very difficult.

For example, repeated attempts to mount worthwhile cultural events like art exhibits in a Cuban art museum in Miami have provoked terrorist attacks by first-generation right-wing Cuban exiles and their followers. In 1996, Miami's Center for the

Fine Arts was forced to cancel an invitation for a lecture by art critic Gerardo Mosquera of Cuba, while the Cantro Vasco restaurant in the heart of Miami's Little Havana was firebombed just for booking Cuba's popular singer Rosita Fornes. In response, People for the American Way launched Miami's "Artsave Project" to bring together both opponents of the Cuban Revolution and opponents of the U.S. trade embargo, as well as prominent patrons of the arts, to combat the right-wing terror campaign and defend artistic freedom of expression.

Despite these efforts for freedom, the intra-community tensions continued. A 1997–1998 art museum exhibition, "Breaking Barriers: Selections from the Museum of Art's Contemporary Cuban Collection," had to be mounted *outside* Miami in Fort Lauderdale's Museum of Art, even though it excluded works by artists still living in Cuba. The curator of the show faced problems caused by his trying to unite different generations of Cuban American artists in a single show. "I wanted to bring all the Cubas together, to forget about who arrived when," he told the press.[3] He more or less succeeded, but not in Miami. His was no small accomplishment in a Cuban community divided by far more than just a stretch of sea separating Cuba from Florida.

Meanwhile, world-class artists from Cuba continued to be sought after throughout the United States. Some regularly exhibited their stunning works in the newly opened Cuban Art Space Gallery at New York City's Center for Cuban Studies, while others were invited to exhibit in leading museums. The days of the U.S. blockade of Cuba—at least in the world of the arts—appeared to be numbered.

Glossary

avant-garde—new or experimental artists or techniques in art

Aztlán—the mythical homeland for Chicanos, said to have been located in the southwestern United States

balsero—a person who tried to leave Cuba by escaping on a raft

banderita—a Mexican hand-crafted object made of tissue paper

barrio—Spanish-speaking neighborhood in a city

Boriquen—the name that Taino Indians gave Puerto Rico; it means Land of the Noble Lord

bulto—a carved statue of a saint or holy figure, such as Christ on the cross

cemi—wood or stone carvings made by Taino Indians said to have spiritual powers

corrido—a ballad that has been passed down from generation to generation

curandera—a female doctor or healer

huelga—the Spanish word for strike

Nuyorican—someone from New York of Puerto Rican descent

objet d'art—an item of artistic value or a knickknack or bauble

Ochassi—the hunter-trapper god in the Santería religion

pachuco—the term for a style of attitude and clothing, especially the zoot suit

Palo Monte—a Congo-based religion popular in Cuba

rasquache—a brazen, garish, outrageous quality

retablo—a painting on flat pieces of wood, metal, or animal skin

Santería—the Afro-Caribbean religion that blends West African beliefs with Christianity

santero—an artist who makes or carves figures of saints

santo—a statue or painted image of a saint

silk screen—a method for making prints by creating an image on a screen of silk and forcing ink through the silk to make a design on paper or other materials under the screen

Tlaloc—the Aztec god of rain

Yemaya—the Yoruban goddess of the sea and protector of fishers

Yoruba—one of the largest ethnic groups in Nigeria; many were brought as slaves to Cuba and the Carribean. Their traditional religion includes the belief in one supreme creator and approximately four hundred lesser gods and spirits

Endnotes

Chapter 1 (uno)

1. Quoting Ramón José López, from Bernadete Finnerty, "Ramón José López Explores His Faith Artistically," <http://www.craftsreport.com/october97/rjlopez.html> (copyright 1997 by Crafts Report). Major sources for this chapter include materials culled from the Internet sites listed in the To Find Out More section of this book, plus the following: James D. Cockcroft, *The Hispanic Struggle for Social Justice* (Danbury, CT: Franklin Watts, 1994); José E. Espinosa, *Saints in the Valleys: Christian Sacred Images in the History, Life, and Folk Art of Spanish New Mexico* (Albuquerque, NM: University of New Mexico Press, 1960); and William Wroth, *Images of Penance, Images of Mercy: Southwestern Santos of the Late Nineteenth Century* (Norman, OK: University of Oklahoma Press, 1991).

2. Quoted in Kathleen Rhames's review of UCLA Fowler Museum show "Cuando hablan los santos" in the *Daily Bruin*, February 21, 1997.

3. *Daily Bruin*, ibid.

4. Quoted in June 16, 1997, press release by the National Endowment for the Arts.

Chapter 2 (dos)

1. Quoted in Francisco Lomelí (ed.), *Handbook of Hispanic Cultures in the United States: Literature and Art* (Houston, TX: Arte Público Press, 1993). Unless otherwise stated, sources for all quotations and biographical sketches in this chapter are from art-show brochures or catalogues. Other major sources include materials culled from the Internet sites listed in the To Find Out More section of this book, plus the following: Rodolfo Acuña, *Occupied America: A History of Chicanos* (New York: Harper & Row, third ed., 1988); John Beardsley and Jane Livingston, *Hispanic Art in the United States: Thirty Contemporary Painters and Sculptors* (New York: Abbeville Press, 1987); Bronx Museum of the Arts, *The Latin American Spirit: Art and Artists in the United States, 1920–1970* (New York: Harry N. Abrams, Inc., Publishers, 1990); Eva Cockcroft, John Pitman Weber, and James D. Cockcroft, *Toward a People's Art: The Contemporary Mural Movement* (Albuquerque, NM: University of New Mexico Press, 1998); Eva Sperling Cockcroft, "From Barrio to Mainstream: The Panorama of Latino Art" in Francisco Lomelí (ed.), *Handbook of Hispanic Cultures in the United States: Literature and Art* (Houston, TX: Arte

Público Press, 1993), pp. 192–217; Eva Sperling Cockcroft and Holly Barnet-Sánchez (eds.), *Signs From the Heart: California Chicano Murals* (Albuquerque, NM: University of New Mexico Press, 1993; copyright by Social and Public Art Resource Center, 1990); James D. Cockcroft, *Diego Rivera* (New York: Chelsea House, 1991) and *Latinos in the Struggle for Equal Education* (Danbury, CT: Franklin Watts, 1996); Hedda Garza, *Frida Kahlo* (New York: Chelsea House, 1994) and *Latinas: Hispanic Women in the United States* (Danbury, CT: Franklin Watts, 1994); and Richard Griswold del Castillo et al. (eds.), *C.A.R.A, Chicano Art: Resistance and Affirmation* 1965–1985 (Los Angeles: Wight Art Gallery, UCLA, 1991).

2. Quoted in Francisco Lomelí (ed.), *Handbook of Hispanic Cultures in the United States: Literature and Art* (Houston, TX: Arte Público Press, 1993), p. 113.

3. For details, see James D. Cockcroft, *Latinos in the Struggle for Equal Education* (Danbury, CT: Franklin Watts, 1996), pp. 34–49.

4. Mujeres Muralistas, Artists' Statement, Chicago Museum of Contemporary Art, 1971.

5. Alicia's statement is available from the Social and Public Art Resource Center (SPARC) in Los Angeles, California.

6. SPARC president Armando Durón's statement is available from SPARC.

7. Gates's statement is available from Latinolink, 1997 <http://www.latinolink.com>.

8. Quoted in Bronx Museum of the Arts, *The Latin American Spirit: Art and Artists in the United States*, 1920–1970 (New York: Harry N. Abrams, Inc., Publishers, 1990), p. 220.

9. Luis Jiménez, Artist's Statement, The Legacy Show, 1997 <http://www.esperanto.com/Legacy>

10. This and later quotations from Moroles are from the Getty Education Institute for the Arts website. <http://www. artsednet.getty. edu/ArtsEdNet/Resources/Moroles/index.html>

11. This and subsequent quotations from Carmen Lomas Garza may be found at the National Museum of American Art's Latino website "del Corazón!" <http://nmaa-ryder.si.edu/ webzine/featpage. htm>

12. Quoted in The Legacy Show, 1997 <http://www. esperanto. com/Legacy>

Chapter 3 (tres)

1. Quoted in Hedda Garza, *Latinas: Hispanic Women in the United States* (Danbury, CT: Franklin Watts, 1994), p. 92. Unless otherwise stated, sources for all quotations and biographical sketches in this chapter are from art-show brochures or catalogues. Other major sources include materials culled from Internet sites listed in the To Find Out More section of this book, plus the following: John Beardsley and Jane Livingston, *Hispanic Art in the United States: Thirty Contemporary Painters and Sculptors* (New York: Abbeville Press, 1987); Bronx Museum of the Arts, *The Latin*

American Spirit: Art and Artists in the United States, 1920–1970 (New York: Harry N. Abrams, Inc., Publishers, 1990); Eva Cockcroft, John Pitman Weber, and James D. Cockcroft, *Toward a People's Art: The Contemporary Mural Movement* (Albuquerque, NM: University of New Mexico Press, 1998); Eva Sperling Cockcroft, "From Barrio to Mainstream: The Panorama of Latino Art" in Francisco Lomelí (ed.), *Handbook of Hispanic Cultures in the United States: Literature and Art* (Houston, TX: Arte Público Press, 1993), pp. 192–217; James D. Cockcroft, *The Hispanic Struggle for Social Justice* (Danbury, CT: Franklin Watts, 1994); I. Curbelo de Díaz, *El Arte de Los Santeros Puertorriqueños/The Art of the Puerto Rican Santeros* (San Juan: Instituto de Cultura Puertorriqueña y Sociedad de Amigos del Museo de Santos, Inc.); and Lucy R. Lippard, *Mixed Blessings: New Art in a Multicultural America* (New York: Pantheon Books, 1990).

2. Holland Carter, *New York Times*, January 2, 1997.

3. Quoted in Bronx Museum of the Arts, *The Latin American Spirit: Art and Artists in the United States 1920–1970* (New York: Harry N. Abrams, Inc., Publishers, 1990), p. 292.

4. Quoted in caption for Plate 26, "Per Capita," in Lucy R. Lippard, *Mixed Blessings: New Art in a Multicultural America* (New York: Pantheon Books, 1990).

Chapter 4 (cuatro)

1. Unless otherwise stated, this and all subsequent quotations are from Marc Zuver (ed.), *CUBA–USA: The First Generation*, cata-

logue from the 1991–1992 exhibition tour (Washington, DC: The Fondo del Sol Visual Arts Center). Other major sources for this chapter include art-show catalogues or brochures, along with materials culled from the Internet sites listed in the To Find Out More section of this book and the following: Luis Cruz Azaceta, Hell: *Luis Cruz Azaceta, Selected Works 1978–1993* (New York: Alternative Museum, 1994); John Beardsley and Jane Livingston, *Hispanic Art in the United States: Thirty Contemporary Painters and Sculptors* (New York: Abbeville Press, 1987); James D. Cockcroft, *Latin America: History, Politics, and U.S. Policy,* Second ed. (Belmont, CA: Wadsworth Publishing/Thomson Learning, 1997), pp. 283–316, 671–682, 713–717; Ileana Fuentes-Pérez et al. (eds.) *Outside Cuba/Fuera de Cuba: Contemporary Cuban Visual Artists* (New Brunswick, NJ: Office of Hispanic Arts, Rutgers University, and Miami, FL: Research Institute for Cuban Studies, University of Miami, 1989); and Arturo Lindsay (ed.) *Santería Aesthetics in Contemporary Latin American Art* (Washington, DC: Smithsonian Institution Press, 1996).

2. Quoted in *ARTnews*, October 1996, p. 94.

3. Enrique Fernandez, "Death, blood and fear eclipse the tropical sun in show of works by Cubans who fled their homeland," *Sun-Sentinel*, October 26, 1997.

Bibliography

Barnett, Alan W. *Community Murals: The People's Art*. New York: Cornwall Books, 1984.

Beardsley, John, and Jane Livingston. *Hispanic Art in the United States: Thirty Contemporary Painters and Sculptors*. New York: Abbeville Press, 1987.

Bronx Museum of the Arts. *The Latin American Spirit: Art and Artists in the United States, 1920–1970*. New York: Harry N. Abrams, Inc., Publishers, 1990.

Cockcroft, Eva, John Pitman Weber, and James Cockcroft. *Toward A People's Art: The Contemporary Mural Movement*. Albuquerque, NM: University of New Mexico Press, 1998.

Cockcroft, Eva Sperling. "From Barrio to Mainstream: The Panorama of Latino Art," in Francisco Lomelí (ed.), *Handbook of Hispanic Cultures in the United States: Literature and Art* (Houston, TX: Arte Público Press, 1993), pp. 192–217.

Cockcroft, Eva Sperling, and Holly Barnet-Sánchez (eds.). *Signs From the Heart: California Chicano Murals.* Albuquerque, NM: University of New Mexico Press, 1993, copyright by Social and Public Art Resource Center, 1990.

Cockcroft, James D. *Diego Rivera.* New York: Chelsea House, 1991.

————. *The Hispanic Struggle for Social Justice.* Danbury, CT: Franklin Watts, 1994.

Drescher, Timothy W. *San Francisco Bay Area Murals: Communities Create their Muses, 1904–1997.* Third ed. St. Paul, MN: Pogo Press, 1998.

Dunitz, Robin J., and James Prigoff. *Street Gallery: Guide to 1000 Los Angeles Murals.* Second ed. Los Angeles: R.J.D. Enterprises, 1998.

Espinosa, José F. *Saints in the Valleys: Christian Sacred Images in the History, Life, and Folk Art of Spanish New Mexico.* Albuquerque, NM: University of New Mexico Press, 1960.

Fuentes-Pérez, Ileana, et al. (eds.). *Outside Cuba/Fuera de Cuba: Contemporary Cuban Visual Artists.* New Brunswick, NJ: Office of Hispanic Arts, Rutgers University, and Miami, FL: Research Institute for Cuban Studies, University of Miami, 1989.

Garduño, Blanca, and José Antonio Rodríguez (Compilers). *Pasión por Frida*. Mexico City: Instituto Nacional de Bellas Arts, 1992.

Garza, Hedda. *Frida Kahlo*. New York: Chelsea House, 1994.

_____. *Latinas: Hispanic Women in the United States*. Danbury, CT: Franklin Watts, 1994.

Goldman, Shifra M. *Dimensions of the Americas: Art and Social Change in Latin America and the United States*. Chicago: University of Chicago Press, 1994.

_____. "A Public Voice: Fifteen Years of Chicano Posters," *Art Journal*, vol. 44, No. 1 (Spring 1994).

Griswold del Castillo, Richard, et al. (eds.). *C.A.R.A, Chicano Art: Resistance and Affirmation 1965–1985*. Los Angeles: Wight Art Gallery, UCLA, 1991.

Lindsay, Arturo (ed.). *Santería Aesthetics in Contemporary Latin American Art*. Washington, DC: Smithsonian Institution Press, 1996.

Lippard, Lucy R. *Mixed Blessings: New Art in a Multicultural America*. New York: Pantheon Books, 1990.

Polkinhorn, Harry, et al. *Visual Arts on the U.S./Mexican Border = Artes plasticas en la frontera Mexico/Estados Unidos*. Calexico, CA: Binational Press; Mexicali, Baja California: Editorial Binacional, 1991.

Steele, Thomas J., S.J. *Santos and Saints: The Religious Folk Art of Hispanic New Mexico*. Santa Fe, NM: Ancient City Press, 1982.

Wroth, William. *Images of Penance, Images of Mercy: Southwestern Santos in the Late Nineteenth Century*. Norman: University of Oklahoma Press, 1991.

Zuver, Marc (ed.). *CUBA–USA: The First Generation*, catalogue from the 1991–1992 exhibition tour. Washington, DC: The Fondo del Sol Visual Arts Center, 1991.

To Find Out More

Books

Cerritos, Joan (ed.). *Comtemporary Artists.* New York: St. James Press, 1996.

Cockcroft, Eva, John Pitman Weber, and James Cockcroft. *Toward A People's Art: The Contemporary Mural Movement.* Albuquerque, NM: University of New Mexico Press, 1998.

Cockcroft, James D. *The Hispanic Struggle for Social Justice.* Danbury, CT: Franklin Watts, 1994.

Cockcroft, James D. *Latinos in the Making of the United States.* Danbury, CT: Franklin Watts, 1995.

Garza, Hedda. *Latinas: Hispanic Women in the United States.* Danbury, CT: Franklin Watts, 1994.

Rasmussen, Waldo (ed.). *Latin American Artists of the Twentieth Century*. Museum of Modern Art, New York: 1993.

Organizations and Online Sites

ARTSEDNET

http://www.artsednet.getty.edu/

Sponsored by the Getty Education Institute for the Arts, this site offers a wealth of art materials, including virtual exhibits and tours as well as online discussions.

"DEL CORAZÓN!"

http://nmaa-ryder.si.edu/webzine/featpage.htm

National Museum of American Art and Texas Education Network created the "del Corazón" site as an online magazine for students and teachers. The site showcases Latino artwork from the museum's collection, and provides resources, activities, and interviews with artists, including Carmen Lomas Garza.

EL MUSEO DEL BARRIO

http://www.elmuseo.org/

This site offers information and images of exhibits and the permanent collection of the museum, including an excellent collection of Puerto Rican *santos*.

LATINOLINK

http://www.latinolink.com

This site provides news, information, and images of all things Latino, including art, music, sports, education, community, and business.

SOCIAL AND PUBLIC ART RESOURCE CENTER MURALS
http://www.sparcmurals.org/
This site is filled with great graphics, artists' statements, links to murals and a tour of the murals, a history of Chicano murals, and related sites.

Index

Page numbers in *italics* indicate illustrations

About the Author

Described by the American Library Association's *Choice* magazine as "an internationally known and distinguished scholar," three-time Fulbright Scholar **James D. Cockcroft** is also an award-winning author of twenty-five books, a poet, and a life-long human rights activist. Besides his works on Latinos, immigration, minorities, Mexico, and hidden history, he has written such works on art as *Diego Rivera* (1991) and the co-authored 1977 classic *Toward a People's Art: The Contemporary Mural Movement* (updated and republished in 1998). His most recent books are *Mexico's Hope: An Encounter with Politics and History*, *Latin America: History, Politics, and U.S. Policy*; and, for Franklin Watts, *Latinos in Béisbol* and *Latinos in the Struggle for Equal Education*.

Jane Canning is a sociologist and freelance journalist who has written extensively on the arts, politics, minorities, and human rights. Dr. Canning also assisted Professor Cockcroft on the recently published Salvador Allende Reader Chile's Voice of Democracy.